Homebuying

TOUGH TIMES,
FIRST TIME,
ANY TIME

Other Titles in the Capital Ideas Series

Homebuying

TOUGH TIMES, FIRST TIME, ANY TIME

Smart Ways to Make a Sound Investment

MICHELE LERNER

CAPITAL IDEAS SERIES

CAPITAL
BOOKS, INC.
Sterling, Virginia

Capital Books, Inc.
P.O. Box 605
Herndon, Virginia 20172-0605

ISBN 13: 978-1-933102-87-0

Library of Congress Cataloging-in-Publication Data

Lerner, Michele.
    Homebuying : tough times, first time, any time : smart ways to make a sound investment / Michele Lerner. — 1st ed.
        p. cm. — (Capital ideas series)
Includes bibliographical references.
    ISBN 978-1-933102-87-0 (alk. paper)
    1. House buying—United States. 2. House buying. I. Title. II. Series.

    HD259.L474 2009
    643'.120973—dc22
                                                                2009014996

Printed in the United States of America on acid-free paper that meets the American National Standards Institute Z39-48 Standard.

First Edition

10 9 8 7 6 5 4 3 2 1

For Mark, Amy, and Sarah,
who always make a home
no matter where we are.

Contents

Acknowledgments

First, I would like to thank my sister, Lisa Schultz, the best research assistant and careful reader anyone could hope for. Her constant support for this project was invaluable.

Next, I want to thank Amy Fries, my excellent editor, who knows just the right questions to ask; and Kathleen Hughes, for giving me this amazing opportunity.

Appreciation is also due to my formal writers group in Washington, D.C., who gave me insights and terrific advice along with encouragement during the writing process; and my informal writing group, Kakki, Donna, and Jeanne, whose e-mails gave me an extra push and burst of enthusiasm when I needed it. My reading group friends deserve thanks, too, for believing that one day I really would write a book instead of just talking about doing it.

Deep thanks also must go to every real estate professional I have interviewed over the years and during the writing of this book. Without their willingness to share their knowledge and their stories, this book would have been impossible to write.

Most of all, though, I need to thank my husband, Mark, my constant companion and my most enthusiastic champion.

Introduction

How the Housing Crisis Changed Homebuying

Joanne and her husband Mike decided it was time to buy a house in the summer of 2005. They were a little worried about their lack of savings, and Mike wished their credit card debt was lower, but they figured once they got into a house they could straighten out their finances. Plus, they assumed that whatever they bought would increase in value anyway. The couple found a lender through the Internet who approved a loan much larger than they expected, without needing a down payment or even proof of their income. Within a year the couple realized they had made a huge mistake, that while the lender told them they could afford to pay $2,500 per month for the mortgage, they hadn't actually done the math themselves. Even with a combined monthly income of $5,500, this mortgage payment required more than 45% of their income, leaving them scrambling to make other payments.

Just a few years later, the residential real estate market has changed dramatically. All mortgage loans now require income and asset verification and are made on the basis of a debt-to-income ratio. Few borrowers can get a mortgage without a down payment, and lenders have introduced stricter standards for credit ratings to ensure that their loans are repaid.

While some potential first-time homebuyers have given up in despair, believing they will be unable to purchase a home, others are aware that mortgages are still available for those who can demonstrate a pattern of financial responsibility.

"A couple of years ago, all you had to have to get a loan was a pulse," says Realtor Jessie L. Brown with Weichert

Realtors, in Charlotte, North Carolina. "The builders loved it and real estate agents loved it, but there was no counseling being done to make sure buyers could actually afford what they were doing."

Mortgage Money Is Still Available

While standards are higher today for financing a home, media reports about the credit crunch have helped to create the false impression that buyers cannot get mortgages these days.

John Holmgren, a mortgage planner with Holmgren & Associates in Oakland, California, says that consumers have a distorted view of the current financial crisis.

"People think that obtaining mortgage financing is impossible because the country is facing a credit crunch, but that is just not true," says Holmgren. "There has been relatively limited demand for mortgages in recent years, so plenty of money is available."

Holmgren says people need to be better qualified than a few years ago when lenders were "ridiculously liberal," but he says this simply represents a return to the way borrowers were qualified a decade ago.

Financial planners and responsible real estate professionals agree that homebuyers today, especially less experienced first-time buyers, are better served by a more realistic loan-approval process.

How We Got Here

To understand how we arrived here, it makes sense to review some recent history about the housing market. Low interest rates and easy credit made it easier for people to buy homes since no one needed to demonstrate a pattern of saving or to make a big down payment, and the monthly payments were relatively low. Government programs meant to encourage homeownership contributed to a loosening of credit and income requirements to qualify for a mortgage. This easy money contributed to skyrocketing demand. As demand shot up, so did home prices. Many renters, terrified that they would be priced out of homeownership forever, jumped in and signed on for mortgages they could not afford. But instead of buying at the lowest possible price, buyers were purchasing homes that were far too costly for their incomes, and lenders were more than willing to sign them up. Many buyers agreed to accept adjustable rate loans, believing that when the interest rates went up they would simply refinance. Lenders and borrowers alike believed that home prices would continue to climb higher and higher.

As prices rose, lenders became more and more willing to lend to even less credit-worthy customers. The lenders believed they could make a profit even if the borrowers defaulted on the loan, since the home value would more than pay off the underlying mortgage if the property had to be sold. Demand for homes was so high that the lenders assumed they could sell a house that had gone into default within a matter of days.

At the same time, investors were buying up securities backed by pools of mortgages, creating ever-greater distance between the borrowers and lenders. In a more old-fashioned real estate market, the lender would actually know the borrower, or at least have all the paperwork that revealed the financial secrets of the borrower. Now the "owners" of the mortgage loans just knew how many loans they owned and for what amount, but not anything about whether the borrower could pay back the money. All these investments depended on home prices continuing to climb.

At the end of 2005, interest rates rose slightly and buyers finally became concerned that home prices were out of control, slowing the demand. Almost overnight, real estate markets around the country flipped from having too few homes to sell to having too many. Buyers left the market and as values dropped and adjustable rate loans reset to higher rates, countless homeowners found themselves unable to sell or refinance their homes and faced foreclosure. Areas around the country where homes were overbuilt and home prices had shot up the fastest, fell harder than others, such as Phoenix, California, South Florida, Las Vegas, and the outer suburbs of cities such as Washington, D.C., and New York City.

The tumbling housing market quickly spread into a massive financial crisis. Bankers and businesses became uncertain of each others' ability to pay back loans and tightened credit terms so severely that builders and other businesses failed. Financial institutions themselves were hit hard, causing some of them to fail. As the recession spread, so did unemployment. In such an environment, many consumers do not have the financial power to buy a home. Many of those who do have the financial ability to enter the housing market lack faith in themselves and the economy.

Marty Frame, general manager of CyberHomes.com, says, "You can track the psychology of this market by just looking at the ebb and flow of mortgage applications from week to week. Interest rates haven't changed that dramatically, but applications go up during weeks when consumer confidence is up."

Where We Go from Here

Consumer doubt undermines the real estate market and does not necessarily match reality. While potential buyers who fear losing their jobs should absolutely not buy a home right now, for others this could be a wise decision. Interest rates remain relatively low, most markets have an abundance of homes for sale, prices are lower than in previous years, and first-time buyers are in the enviable position of not needing to sell their current home in a slow market.

Andy Tolbert, a Realtor with HD Realty in the Orlando, Florida, area, says, "The economic crisis is a double-edged sword. Prices have come down so that average first-time buyers can afford to buy a home. But at the same time, in many areas, property taxes are high and homeowner insurance costs are high. Also, lenders are being less lenient than in the past. But the big benefit to first-time buyers is this—they can take advantage of bargains without worrying about selling their own home."

Frame says the big question for first-time buyers is whether the market has hit bottom yet.

"But if you are a 'ten-year' buyer, intending to stay in the home ten years or longer, then it doesn't matter whether we have hit bottom or not, because you will build equity over time," says Frame. "If you think you will stay in a home for less time than that, maybe you should wait and keep looking for opportunities to buy something way below market value."

While buyers should not expect appreciation of home values in the double-digits, traditionally homes increase in value over time by about 6% per year. In the meantime, the homeowners have the peace of mind that they own property and have the ability to make changes to it as they please, along with the tax benefits of deducting mortgage interest.

Getting Started on the Road to Homeownership

Tolbert says, "The most important tip for first-time buyers: get prequalified for a mortgage first before you look at homes. There's nothing worse than falling in love with a place you can't afford."

The old-fashioned way to buy a house, a method which buyers are returning to today, is to save money for a down payment of 20% or more and then buy a house within the means of the household budget. Neighborhoods of what used to be called "starter homes" were founded on the principle that first-time buyers would purchase a small home, build equity for a few years, then move into a larger home with equity from the first home as the down payment.

Start Saving

Angie Hicks, founder of Angie's List, a consumer group that provides members with information about local contractors and companies, says, "Buyers today need to have their financial house in order before they even think about buying a house. First, they need to have a good understanding of their credit rating and second, they need to have a down payment of 10% to 20% lined up. Saving for that down payment is a challenge people always face, but it is even more important in this market."

Paying off debt (or never getting into debt in the first place) and saving for an emergency fund and a down payment can seem daunting, but accomplishing these tasks can lead to a lifetime of financial health.

David Kerr, a Realtor with ZipRealty, Inc., in the San Francisco area, says, "There's lots of opportunity out there for first-time buyers because prices have dropped by as much as 50% in some places, but buyers really need some down payment. Some have fallen out of the market because they don't have the cash; 00% financing is gone, for the most part."

While financial planners recommend that homebuyers make a down payment of at least 20% so that there is equity in the home from the start, there are still programs in place, particularly loans backed by the government's Federal Housing Administration (FHA), which allow for as little as 3.5% as a down payment. Veterans may qualify for loans backed by the Veteran's Administration, which are available with no down payment at all. Many first-time homebuyers can take advantage of state and local programs that can allow them to obtain a loan with a lower interest rate or a lower down payment, along with potential tax credits. Some of these programs are restricted to buyers with low or moderate incomes or to buyers who work for the government as teachers or policemen, but others are available to all first-time buyers. (First-time buyers are defined as anyone who has not owned a home within the past three years.) Buyers are also allowed to include money provided by relatives for a down payment, as long as they are willing to sign a gift letter, which means they do not expect to be repaid.

Making the choice to purchase a home, or delaying that choice until the time is right to buy requires considerable confidence. Part of the equation in that confidence is purely emotional, feeling mature and responsible enough to do the research required to make decisions and act on them. But confidence also comes from education.

Educating yourself about the homebuying process does not mean you are preparing to enter this complex transaction alone. It simply helps you recognize what to expect from the professionals in the field with whom you will interact. This book functions as a manual to support you along each step of the way from renter to homeowner, providing simple explanations for the complexities associated with buying a home along with lists of the questions you should be asking yourself, your real estate agent, and your lender.

Note: All the homebuyer stories in this book are fiction, based on composite stories told to me by real estate professionals.

CHAPTER ONE

Am I Ready to Buy a Home?

When Marilyn got her first promotion and a raise at the advertising agency where she works, she began to dream big. Marilyn decided to start looking for a condominium to buy in her favorite neighborhood in Chicago, believing her solid instincts would serve her well. That's where she made her first mistake: Marilyn fell in love with a sleek loft-style place with floor-to-ceiling windows, hardwood flooring, granite counters in the kitchen, and an exposed brick wall with a fireplace, never realizing that the place was listed for more than double what she could afford. Before ever discussing her finances with a lender or meeting with a real estate agent who could educate her about the complex real estate market, Marilyn had found her dream home. A home she could not afford to buy.

If you've picked up this book because you are renting a home or living in your mother's basement and think you might be ready to buy a condominium, townhome, or a single-family home, the first thing to do is to stop shopping. First-time buyers are notorious for blithely stepping into open houses and falling in love with a home they cannot afford. The result? Either these buyers finagle a way to finance this purchase and then quickly find themselves strapped for cash, or they walk away from the property and struggle to find something else they can love.

Is Financing Available?

In today's tight economy, first-time buyers will find it more difficult than in previous years to qualify for a loan, which many financial experts think is a good thing. Homebuyers in 2004 and 2005 were frequently approved for a 100% financing loan with an adjustable rate (meaning the monthly payments would change over time) and no proof of income or assets required. Those days are gone. Buyers today need to demonstrate to lenders their ability to earn a steady income, save money, and pay their bills before they can be considered for a loan. But this does not mean, as some pundits proclaim, that "no one can get a loan." Buyers can and do obtain loan approvals every day. It just takes a little preparation.

"Buyers are so afraid that the money is just gone and that mortgages aren't available, but they are," says Antoinette Matisoo, a broker Realtor from Holden, Massachusetts.

Marty Frame, general manager of CyberHomes.com, says that the financial crisis can be a great opportunity for first-time homebuyers, as long as they have the wherewithal to buy and intend to stay in the home for a long time, long enough to recoup the investment.

"Credit qualifications and a down payment are more important than ever before, so if you have good credit, can make a down payment of 20% or more, and intend to stay in the home, buy now," says Frame. "The key message for today's market is that consumers need to save money and borrow from friends and family to be prepared with a down payment to buy a home."

State and local first-time homebuyer programs and loan programs guaranteed by the federal government are also available, which can assist buyers by requiring lower down payments. Loans guaranteed by the FHA (Federal Housing Administration) require a down payment of 3.5%, and veterans and members of the military also have access to VA (Veterans Administration) loans, which are available with no down payment. Another program that many first-time buyers may qualify for is the United States Department of Agriculture (USDA) loan program for rural properties, part of the Rural Development Housing and Community Facilities Programs. This program allows for 100% financing with certain income restrictions.

Rent or Buy?

Renters should start by doing a little Internet research to determine whether renting or buying is the right financial move at any particular time. Real estate markets vary from state to state and even street to street, so deciding when to take the plunge into real estate ownership can be tricky.

Lender web sites such as eloan.com offer quick calculators to help you do the math to decide if buying is worth doing; but keep in mind that lenders *want to make mortgage loans*, so these sites will usually present buying as the better option. Rent vs. own calculators can also be found at SmartMoney.com where the calculation is not influenced by lenders.

The American Bankers Association, ABA.com, provides a general pro/con list for renting versus buying, which should be considered.

Renting pros:

- Requires no maintenance responsibilities.
- Easier to move out of a rental home should you need to relocate or find a better place to live.

Renting cons:

- No building equity (assuming a property increases in value).

- No tax benefits for renters.

- You can't remodel or even change the paint or wallpaper without approval.

- Potential increases in your monthly payments.

Purchasing pros:

- Build equity (assuming eventual increase in property value).

- Take advantage of tax deductions.

- Redecorate to your heart's content.

- Experience a sense of stability and security that comes with being your own landlord.

Purchasing cons:

- Maintenance responsibilities and expenses.

- Property taxes.

- Possibility of being unable to sell the home when you are ready to move.

Jancy Campbell, a broker associate with Real Estate of the Rockies in Boulder, Colorado, recommends that consumers attend a homebuyer's seminar, which educates them about the home-buying process and about the importance of saving money for a down payment, closing costs, and home-maintenance costs.

Homebuyer seminars are offered by local government offices, lenders, and real estate offices. They are often advertised in local newspapers and can be found online by searching for homebuyer seminars in the locality where you want to buy a home.

Campbell suggests that for people who are not sure if they are ready to buy, "There's no obligation in going to see a lender, and I think it's best for consumers to go to two or three to see what programs they offer. They need to figure out what they need to do to prepare, which could take a year or more before they are ready to buy. A good lender or financial planner can run some numbers and discuss what happens if you rent for ten years versus buy. They can also give you some advice about how you can save the money for 10% or 20% down and what the tax savings are if you buy a home."

Job Stability and the Local Real Estate Market

Andy Tolbert, a Realtor with HD Realty in the Orlando, Florida, area, says potential buyers need to be realistic about their finances and their career prospects when making the determination to buy a home.

"You need stability in your life to buy a home," says Tolbert. "If you are job hopping or haven't figured out yet what you want to be when you grow up, then don't buy a house. You could end up with a job with a company that wants you to relocate within six months and have to sell at a loss or not be able to sell at all."

Tolbert says buyers also need to face facts about what they can afford.

"This is a big part of why the country has ended up with so many problems," says Tolbert. "It used to be that first-time buyers went to a community with 'starter homes,' then in three to five years, they moved up. In the last few years, everyone started buying homes at the top, and they were willing to take out funny loans to get there."

One key to making this determination is having a plan. I know, I know, it can be difficult to know what you are eating for dinner tonight, much less where you will be living five years from now. But it's important to have an idea of how long you might stay in a particular location. Buying property should always be a long-term investment, with the intention of staying in the home for five to seven years in order to recoup your initial costs and build some equity. Renters who know they will leave an area within two years or less should probably continue to rent. Renters in areas with falling home prices might make the calculation to wait until the real estate market shifts, but even the most knowledgeable experts have a hard time anticipating when prices or interest rates will begin to rise again.

Brian Fricke, a certified financial planner with Financial Management Concepts in Winter Springs, Florida, and author of *Worry Free Retirement*, says that the exceptional home values created by slumping home prices provide an excellent opportunity for first-time buyers.

"With a fixed-rate thirty-year loan and a down payment, the monthly payments for many buyers will be similar to their rental payment," says Fricke. "If the choice is between paying rent and owning at the same monthly cost, I would advocate for owning."

Fricke says he applies a "five-year rule" to home buying.

"If you choose to buy a home, the odds should be in favor of staying there for at least five years. If you think you will be moving or changing jobs, which could mean leaving the area before five years, it's not necessarily the right time to buy."

For potential buyers worried about whether their home will drop in value after they buy it, Fricke has this advice: "Even today, people who bought their homes ten years ago have value in their homes now, even in a down market. The key is holding onto a property for a long time. Of course, the profits from a home when you sell it are not just based on what you paid, but also on what you put into it in terms of repairs and maintenance, but it is still better than renting. One hundred percent of self-made millionaires own their own homes."

Making a profit on real estate, of course, is also easier when you buy in a down market, such as the one virtually every neighborhood across America is in right now. However, it is impossible for even the most experienced real estate experts to accurately determine when a market has bottomed out. Renters who want the security and freedom of owning their own property, avoiding rent increases, and painting their walls purple should consider buying a home even if prices have dropped a little. Historically, homes in the United States increase in value 6% each year, when you average together the good years with the bad.

David Kerr, a Realtor with ZipRealty in San Francisco, says, "You have to recognize the possibility that the bottom may not have been reached yet. It's hard to know when prices will go up again until it actually happens. But if you are willing to hold property for the long term, it is always the right time to buy. You should also be careful to choose a location where the homes have not dropped a lot in value or where prices have stayed relatively stable because historically those areas will hold their value."

In other words, buying a home in a neighborhood where more than 50% of the homes are foreclosures and are being sold at rock-bottom prices may not be the best investment, since those homes will take longer to rise in value than homes in more stable communities.

Campbell says, "In markets like Boulder, which has a traditionally very strong rental market because of a constant influx of students, buying a home even in this down market could be a very good investment. Even if you don't stay in the house forever, it is likely that you can turn it into an investment property and easily keep it rented."

And, just because you have done the math and think you are not ready to purchase a home right now doesn't mean this is a "forever" decision. Markets change by the week and your circumstances may change, too. Becoming financially prepared to purchase property is a wise move even if you decide to wait before actually buying something.

Credit Reports

Consumers who think they may be ready to purchase a home should obtain a copy of their credit report as much as three to six months before applying for a loan in order to have enough time to correct any potential errors. A credit report will be viewed with the initial loan application, which will provide information on current debts and a credit score (also known as a FICO score, a registered trademark of the Fair Isaac Corporation) that can help determine the applicant's qualification for a loan. Sometimes a credit report will show incorrect information, so it's best to clear up any issues with the credit reporting agencies before beginning to search for a home to purchase. Divorced men and women need to be particularly careful to make sure their credit report does not reflect negative information from an ex-spouse.

Everyone is entitled to one free credit report in each twelve-month period. While there are plenty of websites out there that will give you a "free credit report," they often require you to sign up and pay for a credit-watching service. The only authorized website for requesting an official, free credit report is AnnualCreditReport.com, which includes a combined report from all three authorized credit bureaus.

Discussing your credit report with a lender can be an excellent way to evaluate how to boost your score. But potential buyers who want to get a head start on this should understand how a credit score is generated. According to BankRate.com, credit scores are generated based on the following factors:

- Payment history (35%): Paying on time consistently boosts your score; paying late or less than the minimum hurts your score (a lot).

- Amount you owe and amount of available credit (30%): Credit-reporting agencies look at the level of debt you have and also how much credit is available. Too much available credit is a red flag because the theory is that people are likely to use their available credit. You may feel that having plenty of credit is your security blanket, particularly when you are single and relying on one income; but credit bureaus see thousands of dollars in credit and assume you will be picking up a fur coat next winter.

- Length of credit history (15%): Not only does this look at how long you have had a credit report (not much you can do about this one), but also how long you have had credit with a particular company. In other words, hanging on to your first credit card and diligently making the monthly payments is a good move; better than switching from card to card.

- Mix of credit (10%): Credit agencies think a mix of revolving credit (credit cards) and installment credit (car loans, mortgages) show you can handle credit.

- New credit applications (10%): The agencies take into consideration that someone may be looking for the best mortgage or car loan and therefore have made multiple applications; what they don't like is someone repeatedly applying for more open lines of credit. So don't go to the mall and get 10% off your purchases by picking up new credit cards at Macys, Gap, and Banana Republic. The downward pull on your credit score is not worth the savings.

When reviewing their credit report, consumers should check carefully to be sure all basic information such as name, addresses, birth date, Social Security number, and employer names are correct. They should also look at the list of accounts to make sure they are accurate: those that have been closed should be listed as closed. If anything unfavorable turns up on the report, it is especially important to see if these items are accurate and if they should still be on the report. By law, bankruptcies must be removed from your credit history after ten years, and any other negative information such as a lien, judgment, lawsuit, or arrest record must be dropped after seven years. The credit report will include information about how to dispute incorrect or outdated information.

"Consumers should be very careful in the year or so leading up to the purchase of a home to be sure their credit score is good," says Jason Klein, president of City Line Mortgage in Bethesda, Maryland. "Basically this means not being thirty days late with any bills and making sure that any credit cards are not maxed out. If you have a card with a $15,000 limit, and you have used all that credit, it can negatively impact your score. You can either try to pay down the credit card, or consolidate the debt onto another card with a higher limit to free up the credit on that card, or even call the credit card company and ask them to extend the credit limit to a higher amount."

Fricke says the best way to improve your credit score is to find a loan officer who knows how to make your credit rating more attractive to lenders. It can take six months or longer to significantly impact a credit score, depending on individual circumstances.

"Your score goes up based on having a low outstanding balance on your credit line," says Fricke. "So it's better to owe $10,000 on a $30,000 line of credit rather than $10,000 on a $10,000 line of credit, even though it is the same amount of debt."

Jessie L. Brown III, a Realtor with Weichert Realtors in Charlotte, North Carolina, learned the rules about credit scores and what lenders are looking for so he can work with potential buyers to improve their credit scores.

"I try never to send people to a credit repair program," says Brown. "I would rather help them myself. I tell them to get a new credit card, which could send your score up by 100 points or more. It looks good that someone wants to give you credit. I also recommend that people keep their balance to less than 20% of the credit limit. Everyone should have two credit cards and use them. Don't just hold the card, you need to show that you are financially responsible and will make on-time payments."

An online tool for consumers that can help them see the impact of their credit score on their potential mortgage payments is called the Mortgage Simulator, TrueCredit.com/Mortgage. This mortgage calculator, for a nominal fee, incorporates a consumer's credit score with a personalized loan-rate analysis with mortgage rates updated daily. Most important, this calculator has a "What If" tool, which helps users determine how changing various factors such as their credit score or their debt-to-income ratio can improve their borrowing power.

How Much Should You Spend?

In addition to reviewing your credit score, income and assets, lenders determine a debt-to-income ratio as part of the loan-approval process. In other words, this will be the combined costs of all of your minimum monthly payments versus your gross monthly income. Your gross monthly income includes not just your salary. It also includes other sources of income such as alimony, Social Security, pensions, or an estimated percentage of bonuses or commissions.

Fricke says, "The old-fashioned way of thinking about buying a home is making a comeback: it used to be people spent 2.5 to three times their salary for their home purchase, and paid at least 10% to 20% of the price as a down payment.

If they couldn't save that much, they asked their parents and got a gift letter from them. In addition, you were supposed to have a ratio of 28% of your gross income spent on housing costs and a maximum of 36% of your gross income on total debt. To budget for a house, you should start with the old-fashioned ratios and then listen to your gut about how much to spend. What the lender says is not necessarily what you will be comfortable with. It's really okay to spend less than the lender says you can spend. Obviously, given our current situation, lenders don't know everything!"

Klein says that the highest back-end ratio (the combined mortgage payment and minimum monthly payments for any other debt) should be no larger than 45% of the gross monthly income.

"But these ratios are really a moving target," says Klein. "Borrowers with excellent credit scores and lots of down payment money can sometimes have a higher back-end ratio."

While a mortgage lender will tell you the maximum loan for which you can qualify, this doesn't mean that you should immediately look for a home in that price range. Determining how much to spend on housing costs should be part of a "big picture" financial plan. Just because your lender says you can afford a $600,000 mortgage doesn't mean you won't feel the pinch when the payment is due each month.

Tolbert says, "First look at your budget, then discuss what you can qualify for. For instance, if someone comes in and tells me they want their monthly payments at a level that correlates with a $150,000 home, then that's what we look at. If the bank says they can qualify for $200,000, then I'll tell them that they have a little leeway, but that they should really stick with what they are comfortable paying."

Financial planners warn that some lenders encourage consumers to borrow every penny of what they are qualified for because their mission is to make loans. But the recent debacle of homeowners getting behind on their payments and loans entering foreclosure has made many lenders more wary about overestimating the financial strength of borrowers. Financial planners recommend using a wide-angle lens to look at the entirety of your financial situation when determining how much to spend.

For example, if your favorite activity every weekend is playing golf, then you need to include the monthly cost for the sport in your budget. A lender won't do that for you, because golf (believe it or not!) is not considered a necessary expenditure.

Greg Smith, a financial planner from Reston, Virginia, with the Wise Investor Group, says that he has heard the number 28% tossed around as the percent of the monthly gross income which should be spent just on housing costs.

"That number is basically just picked out of thin air," says Smith. "If someone makes $30,000 per year, there would be almost no way they would be able to keep up with today's housing costs spending just 28%. But for someone making $5,000,000 per year, spending 28% of their monthly income on a mortgage would be absurdly high."

Mark Atherton, a certified financial planner with Ticknor, Atherton and Associates in Reston, Virginia, says that deciding how large a mortgage to take on is based on an individual's risk tolerance just like any other investment. Conservative borrowers will want to spend a smaller portion of their income on their mortgage payments than those who are willing to bet their income will rise fast enough to make high mortgage payments more comfortable in future years. Clearly, few potential homebuyers today can count on rising incomes or bonuses during the recession. Home purchasers would be wise to err on the side of conservatism in this market.

Atherton says, "Consumers need to think about the stability of their jobs, and they need to plan for potential changes such as a growing family or a disability."

Clearly, life throws curve balls to everyone, so it's impossible to predict what good or bad events may occur that will change your life. In recessionary times, the risks of losing a job or just having your hours cut and your income reduced are possibilities for nearly everyone. Most people assume they have a stable job, but if you have recently entered a new career or there are rumors about lay-offs flying around your office, this might not be the time to jump into the heavy financial commitment of buying a home. Additionally, making sure you have sufficient savings in the bank should be part of your consideration of taking on the responsibility of a home loan. In other words, take a long and sober look at your overall financial picture and make an educated guess at what the future may hold.

Fricke says that buyers should set realistic expectations and then spend time getting ready financially for buying a home.

"Lots of people dream of owning a big house with a big yard in the perfect neighborhood, but that's rare in a first home," says Fricke. "I tell people to get in the game and start building equity in your first home so you can move onto that perfect home. Before that, though, you need to get ready financially. People either have no money saved or they have it all in retirement accounts. I recommend that people put in the maximum amount of money in a retirement account that the company will match, but also make sure you are saving for an emergency fund and a down payment."

Fricke says, under some circumstances, companies will allow employees to borrow up to one-half the balance from a 401K account, but he does not recommend this unless absolutely necessary.

"You have to repay the money with interest through payroll deductions within five years," says Fricke. "If you leave the company or don't pay it back, you have to treat it as income for taxes and pay a 10% penalty. So you really don't want to do this if you can help it. The better option is to make sure you are saving money outside a 401K and an IRA."

Single buyers should consider the implications financially if they think they may marry or move in with a partner during the first few years of homeownership. Selling a property within a year or two of purchase can result in a loss, so it's important to carefully choose a home which can meet your needs in future years, not just today.

Klein makes certain that his borrowers understand that housing costs are not simply the mortgage principal and interest payments, but that they also include taxes, insurance, and condominium or homeowner association fees. Property taxes are normally part of the listing information for a property, along with condominium and homeowner association fees, which vary widely according to the type of property and community amenities. Single-family homes that are not part of a homeowner's association will not require such fees, but the owners may need to pay separately for trash pick-up or other items covered by a homeowner's association.

While lenders and online mortgage calculators take into account taxes, insurance, and homeowner association fees, they leave out utilities and the possibility of an increase in insurance costs, along with other bills associated with homeownership such as necessary repairs or remodeling.

Potential buyers need to think about how long they intend to stay in a home and compare potential monthly costs between their current rented residence and a home they would buy, not forgetting to include things like maintenance costs or possibly condominium fees. Of course, a final decision on whether renting or buying is right for you requires moving onto the next step, meeting with a lender and facing up to the hard financial facts.

✓ **CHECKLIST**

- ❏ Determine whether now is the time to buy a home.
- ❏ Review your entire household budget.
- ❏ Make a long-term plan; think about how long you want to stay in your current job and your current location.
- ❏ Obtain your free credit report and review it.

CHAPTER TWO

Financing for First-Time Buyers

A young couple living in Orlando, Florida, was determined to buy their first home when they saw that home prices had dropped in their area, even though they didn't have much money saved. They initially worked with a lender who promised them they could qualify for a loan program with a low-interest-rate mortgage and all the down-payment money and closing costs provided by the seller. After Joanne and Steve found a townhome they thought they could afford, they went back to the lender, who told them that the program allowing sellers to pay all upfront costs no longer existed. Additionally, the lender told them their credit scores were too low to qualify for a conventional loan.

Happily, the lender was able to help them figure out how to pay off some of their debts and improve their credit scores. Both Joanne and Steve took on part-time jobs on the weekend for a few months to generate extra income, while cutting their spending in order to pay off their credit card debt. In the meantime, they continued to look for property and speak regularly with their lender. Their real estate agent and lender helped them arrange financing for a duplex, allowing them to buy a home for themselves and rent the adjacent home to generate income. This couple's persistence and the expertise and creativity of their real estate professionals allowed them to achieve their goal of homeownership.

Meet with a Lender

As part of the decision making about purchasing a home, potential buyers should plan to meet with a lender to determine how much they can afford to spend on housing costs. In today's economy, many potential buyers fear they will be unable to qualify for a loan. Media reports of people needing credit scores above 800 and a minimum down payment of 20% as requirements for loan approval are greatly exaggerated. But these reports do demonstrate the reality of today's mortgage market: potential borrowers will be evaluated on the basis of their credit scores, income, assets, and liabilities. But, truly, if the numbers are right, the loan will be approved.

Angie Hicks, founder of Angie's List, a consumer group that provides members with information about local contractors and companies, says that meeting as early as possible with a lender will help first-time buyers understand where they need to be in terms of their credit, income, and savings in order to buy the house they want.

"A lender may say that the potential borrowers simply cannot qualify for a loan, but a good lender can map out a strategy for saving and improving their credit score so that they can qualify at some point in the future," says Hicks. "Buyers need to save so that they can make a down payment of 10% to 20%. How to save that extra money depends on the buyer's individual circumstances. Sometimes it takes a second job for some period of time or even living with parents longer in order to save on expenses."

Serious homebuyers must obtain a preapproval letter for a loan, since, particularly during a recession and credit crunch, almost no sellers will consider accepting an offer without proof that the buyer can obtain a mortgage.

First-time buyers, even those who consider themselves financially savvy, should start the process of a home purchase by finding a reputable mortgage lender. No, not "Joe's Mortgages" found on the Internet. There should be several priorities when looking for a lender:

- Find a local lender, someone you can communicate with easily and meet in person. A personal connection can be invaluable if any problems arise. Some homebuyers prefer to find a real estate agent first, who can then recommend a trustworthy lender. This is almost a chicken-or-egg proposition: you can find an agent who can recommend a lender; or you can find a lender who can recommend an agent. The process is pretty much the same. The main thing is that you want to assemble a team of people that can work with each other, and, most importantly, work with you.

- Ask friends, colleagues, neighbors, and preferably, recent homebuyers, to recommend a lender or a real estate agent. Interview several of these lenders or Realtors by phone before making an appointment to get an idea of whether you'll be comfortable revealing every intimate financial detail of your life. That's right, both the good and the bad must be shared with your lender. Your Realtor will need to have a summary of this information, too, in order to help you find an appropriate property to buy.

- Try to find a lender or agent experienced in working with first-time buyers. While a reputable lender or Realtor may come highly recommended, these professionals might function best when working with high-end veterans of the housing market, rather than with a buyer who needs plenty of hand-holding.

- After interviewing several lenders or Realtors by phone, make an appointment to meet with them in person and choose which one to work with.

- An important note: if you opt to buy a new home, builders often offer incentives such as paying closing costs or including such optional features as a finished basement to buyers who use the builder's preferred lender and settlement company. Buyers should compare the loan offer from the builder's lender with a loan offer from another lender. Most often, the financial incentive of having your closing costs paid will make the builder's loan preferable, but it's still wise to make that comparison before agreeing to accept the loan.

Andy Tolbert, a Realtor with HD Realty in the Orlando, Florida, area, says, "First-time buyers need to deal with a mortgage company that works with the FHA (Federal Housing Administration) program, and they need to find a lender with plenty of experience. It doesn't cost any more to deal with someone with twenty years of experience than with someone new to the profession."

Diane Williams, an associate broker with Weichert Realtors in Springhouse, Pennsylvania, reiterates the importance of working with a reputable, reliable lender.

"I've had buyers come close to the settlement date and be frustrated because the lender they found on the Internet says the program they thought was locked in is no longer available," says Williams.

Jason Klein, president of City Line Mortgage in Bethesda, Maryland, says that at the first meeting with potential buyers, he has them complete a loan application, including getting information on their income and assets.

Klein says, "Then we can almost immediately determine the maximum that they can afford for a property either as a dollar amount for the purchase price or as a monthly mortgage payment. After we determine how much they can qualify for, we talk about the loan programs that are available to meet their needs."

Klein says that most first-time buyers are unfamiliar with the loan products that are available and also have no feeling for what the monthly loan payment will be or for the process of going from the loan application to the approval to the closing. To start the process, borrowers need to be prepared for their first lender meeting by compiling the following documentation on income and assets:

- Bank statements for all accounts, including retirement funds, stocks, bonds, mutual funds, checking and savings accounts (print these if you bank online).

- A recent pay stub for thirty days of income, which also shows year-to-date income.

- Proof of other income such as a second job, alimony, or bonuses.

- W-2 forms for the past two years.

- Two years of your job history with addresses for all employers.

- Two years of residential addresses and landlord information.

- If you are self-employed, you will also need the most recent two years of tax returns.

- Social Security number to check credit reports.

- Some lenders will request a list of all creditors, although this can also be determined from your credit report.

- Driver's license for additional identification.

"A strong loan commitment can be made based on the income and assets and a check of the credit report, but the final loan approval must be made for a specific property after an appraisal of that property," says Klein.

In other words, a preapproval is not a guarantee of a loan, but it goes a long way in giving buyers peace-of-mind that they can finance their home purchase.

According to Klein, typically the best interest rates are available to borrowers with a credit score of 680 or higher, but homebuyers with lower scores can often compensate for the score with a larger down payment. They can also qualify for loan programs with slightly higher interest rates. Experienced lenders can advise buyers on the best way to raise their credit score.

Borrowers concerned about affording their monthly mortgage payment often rely on the tax benefit of deducting mortgage interest to offset their monthly payments. Klein recommends that borrowers talk to a tax accountant to get a feel for what the tax write-off will be. They can adjust their tax withholdings accordingly so that they keep more of their monthly paycheck rather than waiting for a tax refund.

First-Time Buyer Programs

Potential buyers should also be sure to ask their lender and their real estate agent about special programs for first-time buyers. First-time buyers are identified by the federal government as anyone who has not owned property within the previous three tax years. Many state and local governments offer a tax credit for first-time homebuyers, along with down-payment and closing-cost assistance. Some of these programs are restricted by the income level of the buyers and/or the price of the property. See the appendix for more information.

For first-time buyers, the biggest obstacle to purchasing a home is usually accumulating a down payment, especially when you are living on one income. While funds are needed for closing costs and moving costs, financing programs are available that require a smaller down payment than traditional loans. For example, mortgage loans offered by the government-backed Federal Housing Administration (FHA), require only a 3.5% down payment, some of which can be from a gift from relatives. (FHA.gov)

John Holmgren, a mortgage planner with Holmgren & Associates in Oakland, California, says, "Conventional loans usually require a 10% down payment, but under certain circumstances, especially with good credit or a high income, buyers can get away with a lower down payment. If you have 20% or more to put down, you can get a loan even with just okay credit."

In this current buyers' market, particularly in areas where sellers are experiencing extreme difficulty selling their homes, buyers can often negotiate for closing-cost assistance, which can reduce the need for cash savings.

Ken Fisher, an attorney from Cleveland, Ohio, suggests that in addition to taking advantage of government-incentive programs to buy a home, buyers should investigate the possibility of seller financing.

"Buyers may want to look into a 'purchase money mortgage' or 'seller financing,'" says Fisher. "This is when a seller/owner is willing to take back a second mortgage for someone who wants to buy but doesn't have enough for a substantial down payment. Sometimes a seller will even do an 80% finance if the buyers make a 20% down payment. This is different from a lease/option because the title transfers right away to the buyers. A seller might be willing to do this if they own the house free and clear with no mortgage or if they have inherited a house with no mortgage. It all depends on the seller's situation, but there are definitely sellers willing to do this under certain circumstances, which could help a buyer who can't qualify for a conventional loan."

FHA and VA Loans

While obtaining seller financing may be rare, first-time buyers in today's market frequently opt for FHA or VA (Veterans Affairs) loans because they require a low down payment or no down payment and have less-strict requirements on credit scores and debt-to-income ratios. VA loans are restricted to current members of the military, veterans, and their spouses. More information about the availability of VA loans and their restrictions can be found at HomeLoans.va.gov.

Holmgren says, "FHA loans had fallen to just 1% to 2% of the mortgage loan market a few years ago, but now more than half of all loans are FHA loans."

Realtor Jessie Brown, with Weichert Realtors in Charlotte, North Carolina, says that one reason that FHA and VA loans are so popular in this market is that their rules are less strict about credit scoring.

"As long as you have a credit score of 580 or better, you should be able to qualify," says Brown. "Even if you have collections against you, as long as they are one year old or older, FHA should accept you."

Tolbert says that FHA loan requirements, though, are less lenient in today's market than they were in the past. She says that even though the FHA does not have a published minimum credit score, it can be really tough to qualify for a loan if your score is under 580, although you can compensate with a bigger down payment.

"Good credit is generally considered to be a score of 620 or higher," says Tolbert. "But it is important to understand that the reasons for a low credit score matter. For instance, blemishes either need to make sense (such as a car accident which kept you out of work for two months, not overspending at Christmas); or they need to be far enough in the past. Even bankruptcies and foreclosures can be overcome with time."

Tolbert stresses that one of the worst blemishes in the eyes of lenders is a judgment for not making child-support payments.

"First, no one likes a deadbeat; but second, if you get thrown in jail for not paying child support, then you can't pay your mortgage," says Tolbert.

While FHA and VA loans have more lenient credit requirements than conventional loans, they are limited to homes priced at a certain level. The level, set by the government, varies according to the average home prices in the area. Nationwide, the FHA loan limit is $417,000, but the limits are raised on a sliding scale in areas with more expensive homes. Loan limits in the most expensive areas of the country, such as Washington, D.C., San Francisco, New York City, Los Angeles, and Jackson, Wyoming, are now capped at $729,750. Borrowers can search on the FHA web site (FHA.gov) by county to see the limits for their area, although most Realtors and lenders have this information at their fingertips.

David Kerr, a Realtor with ZipRealty in San Francisco, says FHA loans are restricted in other ways besides home prices.

"Not all homes qualify for the FHA program," says Kerr. "For instance, a lot of foreclosures can't be financed through FHA because the property must be in livable condition."

Borrowers who want to purchase a home with an FHA loan or a VA loan need to be sure the property they are interested in will qualify for the program. The listing agent for the property (or the builder, if this is a new home development) will be able to determine whether these types of loans are allowable for the purchase.

Conforming Loans and Jumbo Loans

While the assumption is often made that first-time home-buyers will be purchasing an affordable home at the lower end of the housing market for their area, first-time buyers can be looking at homes in any price range. It just depends on their income and assets.

Mortgage financing for more expensive homes, though, can be harder to obtain. Just as FHA loans are limited by the price of homes in certain areas, the Federal Housing Finance Agency (FHFA) limits loans that can be purchased by Fannie Mae and Freddie Mac (government-sponsored entities that buy loans from other lenders) to $417,000 in most areas of the country, with an upper limit of $625,500 in the most expensive areas.

Loans that meet these limits are known as "conforming loans," while those that are above the limit are called "jumbo loans." Interest rates for jumbo loans are generally higher than for conforming loans because the loans cannot be sold to Fannie Mae and Freddie Mac and are therefore considered higher-risk loans.

Holmgren says, "There's less availability for jumbo loans of over $625,500. In this market, you really need a 20% down payment and higher credit scores than in the past—of at least 680. There are fewer loan products out there in that price range."

Fixed-Rate vs. Adjustable-Rate Loans

Determining the appropriate loan program should be an individualized decision made between you and your lender, based on personal financial circumstances and your comfort level. There is no one-size-fits-all when it comes to loan programs.

By far the most popular loans in the current real estate market are fixed-rate loans, primarily because consumers saw the dangers of adjustable-rate loans when home values dropped. Homeowners who had anticipated being able to refinance their loans before the payments rose too high found they were unable to do so when the value of their homes plummeted. They lost equity in the home and lenders could not make new loans on the property.

Some borrowers opt for an adjustable-rate loan in order to save money on the interest rates. Adjustable rate mortgages (ARMs) come with a fixed-interest rate only for a certain period of time, such as one year or two years, then the interest rate will adjust. When interest rates change, ARM monthly payments increase or decrease at intervals determined by the lender and agreed to by the borrower. Most ARMs do have a cap, which means that monthly payments cannot rise above that level.

A problem with these loans is that borrowers often assume they will make more money or their home will increase in value so they can refinance when the rates change. But given the rocky job market and, as we've seen, the stagnant or falling home values in many areas, it's risky to make assumptions about future raises and a quick increase in equity.

It's important to ask as many questions as it takes until you completely understand the loan program before making a commitment. In particular, borrowers who choose an adjustable-rate loan or a fixed-rate loan with an interest-only period for some length of time need to look at the future potential payments. A wide variety of adjustable-rate loans are available, so it's crucial to know what the maximum payment could be in any year of the loan and to estimate if that payment will be affordable for you. Fixed-rate loans offer protection against a potential increase in interest rates.

Interest-rate adjustments on ARMs can mean a significant change in the monthly payment. For example, a $400,000 mortgage, fixed at 7%, costs $2,661 per month for principal and interest, while that same loan at 5% interest costs $2,147— a difference of more than $500 per month.

In addition to understanding adjustable- versus fixed-rate loans, first-time buyers need to make sure their lender explains some of the other costs associated with obtaining a mortgage.

Private Mortgage Insurance (PMI)

"Buyers who make a down payment of less than 20% must normally pay Private Mortgage Insurance (PMI), which protects the lender, not the consumer," says Holmgren. "PMI payments are not always tax deductible, and, especially for large loans, can be a substantial monthly expense. There are two options for borrowers to avoid monthly PMI payments, if they cannot make a 20% down payment."

One option is "lender-paid mortgage insurance," offered by many lenders, which allows the borrower to wrap the PMI into the loan by paying a slightly higher interest rate. The PMI then becomes a tax-deductible expense along with the rest of the mortgage-interest payments for all borrowers. (Standard PMI premiums recently became tax-deductible for some borrowers who meet the income-limitation requirements.)

Another option is "single premium mortgage insurance," which is paid upfront at the closing, a payment of about 2.5% to 3.5% of the loan. This lump sum can sometimes be financed as part of the loan, and other times buyers can negotiate with the seller to finance this as a seller credit at closing.

Discount Points

Borrowers can pay extra at the settlement table, known as "discount points" or "points" to bring down the interest rate to make the monthly payments more affordable. It's important when comparing loans to know whether a quoted interest rate includes points or not. Borrowers may think they are getting a great low-interest mortgage rate but they should know that they may need to pay more upfront to get that rate. Generally, these points are calculated to be 1% of the total loan amount, or $4,000 on a $400,000 loan.

Buyers with enough cash may want to discuss the viability of paying points with their lender, or consider making a larger down payment. A lender can discuss the pros and cons of both decisions, which depend on each person's circumstances such as her age, her income, any anticipated increase in income such as a bonus or a raise, and her overall investment strategy.

Most loan offers are quoted with an interest rate and points, often 1, 2, or 3 points. The borrower can decide which loan to accept, including asking for a loan with zero points. A shift in the number of points will change the interest rate.

Borrowers who have little cash and need the lowest possible closing costs will want to choose a zero-point option. Borrowers with more savings and a greater concern about their monthly payments may want to pay more points at the closing to keep their interest rate as low as possible.

One more factor should be considered when thinking about paying points. If you plan to stay in your home for a long time, as most buyers today do, it may be worthwhile to pay extra points at the closing so that you can take advantage of a lower interest rate for the length of your loan.

A lender can quickly do the calculations comparing your monthly payments and upfront costs at a variety of interest rates and points to see what best suits your needs.

Bankrate.com provides the following example: If you choose a thirty-year fixed mortgage of $165,000 at 6% with zero points, you would have a monthly principal and interest payment of $989. If you pay 2 points at closing ($3,300), you can bring the interest rate down to 5.5%, with a monthly payment of $937, a savings of $52 per month. It would take sixty-four months to earn back the $3,300 spent upfront through the lower payments. If you know you will own the house for more than sixty-four months (or five and one-half years), then you save money by paying the points.

Interest-Only Loans

First-time buyers should discuss in depth the various available loan programs for their particular situation with their lender, who should offer a variety of potential loan scenarios and identify the advantages and disadvantages of each product. Interest-only loans, which allow borrowers to pay only the interest for a certain number of years in order to lower the monthly payments, were popular at the height of the real estate boom when home prices were skyrocketing and buyers needed such loans to afford to buy at all. The principal will not be paid down during the interest-only period of the loan, after which the monthly payments will rise significantly because they will include the full principal-and-interest payments on the property. Interest-only loans are much harder to find in today's mortgage market.

"I don't recommend interest-only loans to first-time buyers because if the property drops in value, even if it is only by 1%, then the buyers could owe more money on the loan than the home is worth," says Klein. "Interest-only loans are all right if people are disciplined and pay additional money toward the principal, but typically first-time buyers are stretching to make the payments so they are not as likely to do this. It's important that homebuyers understand everything about the loan they choose."

Closing Costs

A detailed estimate of your closing costs will be given when you complete a loan application for a particular property, but you should ask your lender for an approximate guess at your closing costs at your initial meeting so you know how much cash you may need to buy a home.

Closing costs vary from state to state, but are generally 3% to 5% of the sales price of the home. Your lender and your real estate agent can give you an idea, based on your local market, about the likelihood of negotiating for your seller to pay these costs.

Locking-in a Loan

You should ask your lender about when to a "lock-in" a loan rate, which means that the interest rates and points you agreed on will remain the same for a certain period of time. Usually lock-in agreements last for fifteen to sixty days, allowing you time to go to settlement on the house. If you or your lender are concerned about interest rates going up, you can agree to lock-in the rate as soon as your loan is approved.

Loan Approval

Obtaining a preapproval for a mortgage makes the final loan approval faster, since the lender or mortgage broker will already have in place the required documentation of your income and assets. The final loan approval will be based on your qualifications and an appraisal of the property to make sure it has value equal to or more than the mortgage.

Loan approvals vary widely because of individual circumstances, taking anywhere from twenty-four hours to three or four weeks. Typically, a loan approval will take seven to ten days.

Prepayment Penalties

The majority of mortgage loans do not have a prepayment penalty, which would require a payment if you pay off the loan or refinance it during a certain timeframe, such as six months of interest payments if the loan is paid off within the first five years of ownership. Generally, prepayment penalties are associated with loans made to less qualified borrowers who must accept a mortgage with less favorable terms. It is important to check with your lender to be certain that your loan doesn't have such a penalty.

Questions to Ask Your Lender

- Is this an adjustable-rate or fixed-rate loan?
- What is the interest rate?
- What is the minimum down payment required for approval on this loan?
- Can you give me some comparisons of loans with different points and interest rates?
- Will I need to pay for Personal Mortgage Insurance (PMI)?
- What will my entire monthly payment be, including principal, interest, insurance, and taxes?
- What should I expect to pay for closing costs?
- Can I "lock-in" the interest rate while I look for a home? For how long?
- How long should it take to get final approval on the loan once I have found a house to buy?
- Is there a prepayment penalty on the loan? (Right now it may seem outrageous to think you would be able to pay off thousands of dollars at once, but it is possible that a windfall could come your way. Or, more likely, that you may want to refinance the loan at some future date.)

Lenders are required to provide a "good-faith estimate" within three days of applying for a loan, which will estimate the fees you will need to pay at settlement. This good-faith estimate will be given after you have found a home and completed the full application for a loan based on the contract price for the property, not at the initial consultation with the lender when you are applying for preapproval for a loan. The difference is that the actual loan application will be based on the actual sales price of the house, not a ballpark figure. Closing costs are generally 3% to 5% percent of the sales price of the home; but, depending on the market, many buyers are able to negotiate with the sellers to have them contribute all or some of these costs.

During the entire process from applying for a loan to approval to settlement, it's vital for buyers to stay in touch with their lender. Either you or your lender should initiate communication every few days just to be certain there are no missing documents or problems with the loan.

✓ CHECKLIST

❑ Get recommendations for a lender and Realtor from friends and colleagues.

❑ Interview several lenders or Realtors, and choose one to work with.

❑ Gather documentation for your loan application.

❑ Review your credit report with your lender to determine if you need to take steps to improve your credit score.

❑ Ask about special programs in your area for first-time buyers.

❑ Ask questions and more questions of your lender until you understand your loan, especially if you opt for an adjustable-rate or interest-only loan.

❑ Review your Good Faith Estimate to be sure you understand your expenses at settlement and that you will have the resources to pay the closing costs.

CHAPTER THREE

Lease-to-Own Agreements

When Melissa and John got engaged, they hoped to buy a home that they could move into as soon as they were married. They each had been trying to save money since they started working, but because they were both paying off student loans and lived in a city where the rents were high, they hadn't accumulated much. Melissa's parents were willing to help them with a down payment, so the couple decided to go to a lender and see what they might be able to afford. Even with their savings and a gift from their parents, Melissa and John needed to save a little longer in order to buy a home they wanted and make a down payment of at least 3.5%. The couple was worried that prices might rise again before they were able to save enough, so the lender suggested they look into a lease-option or rent-to-own arrangement, which would allow them to move into a place they wanted to buy and have some of their monthly rent credited toward the down payment. They found a condominium in a neighborhood where some of their friends lived and were able to negotiate a twelve-month rent-to-own agreement with the help of a lawyer.

What Are Rent-to-Own Agreements?

These are names for programs that allow renters to combine renting with an option or agreement to buy a property. Such agreements vary from state to state and include "rent-to-own," "lease-option," or "lease-to-own," but the basic premise is the same: renters and sellers negotiate an agreement for the option to purchase a property at a specified time and price. An alternative arrangement is an actual binding contract to buy the property.

Realtor Andy Tolbert, with HD Realty in Orlando, Florida, says, "There are basically lease-option and lease-purchase programs, which are two different things. A lease-option means you have the option to buy when the lease ends (in a year or whatever the lease length is), but you are not required to buy at that time. A lease-purchase says that you will buy the home at the end of the lease, and there are penalties that can be applied if you don't buy."

Attorney Jim Savitz, with Village Settlements in Gaithersburg, Maryland, says the lease-option arrangement is similar to a "first right of refusal," with the renters deciding at the end of the lease period whether they want to buy it or not without any obligation to buy the property.

Some sellers actively market their homes as a lease-to-own property, while others are willing to negotiate an agreement but do not necessarily advertise this. Some new developments, particularly condominiums, are also actively marketing their homes as rent-to-own properties to entice consumers who might otherwise continue to rent. Some websites with rent-to-own property listings across the country can be found at the end of this chapter. Potential buyers interested in a lease-to-own arrangement can also ask their Realtors about properties available with these options and can search online for rent-to-own properties in their area.

Why Opt for a Rent-to-Own Arrangement?

There are several reasons why renters might be interested in entering into a rent-to-own arrangement. Renters who will find such an agreement most appealing are those who have identified a property they want to buy but need more time to save money for a down payment or to repair their credit.

Ken Fisher, an attorney from Cleveland, Ohio, says, "Lease-options can be very valuable to buyers, and I think we'll be seeing more of these because the arrangement is not contingent on qualifying for a loan. If you can't qualify for a conventional loan, this may be a good way to get into a house while the prices are affordable."

(If you still can't qualify for a loan at the end of a rent-to-own arrangement, the arrangement will be void. Penalties may apply depending on how the agreement was written.)

Many renters who have watched home prices plummet in their neighborhood have looked at the market with both excitement and fear. On the one hand, they may think that homes are finally reaching a price point where they can consider becoming homeowners. On the other hand, they've watched homeowners lose the equity they thought they had in their homes, so they don't want to be in the same boat. But timing the market to buy at the bottom is a risky game. A lease-to-purchase arrangement offers the buyers a little extra time to watch the market.

John Holmgren, a mortgage planner with Holmgren & Associates in Oakland, California, says, "Renters sometimes decide to go into a rent-to-own arrangement because they are afraid the price will go up on a house, and they want to lock in a price. But they also want the option of not buying it in case the price drops or they change their minds at the end of the lease. Consumers are watching to see if the market has bottomed out, so it might make sense for some of them to do a rent-to-own."

Tolbert says that the main benefit of a rent-to-own agreement is that it allows consumers time to fix their credit, let a bankruptcy be older on the credit report, or, if they have started a business, to allow two years worth of self-employment income to build up and create a track record, which lenders can use when they approve a loan.

"Another benefit to renters," says Tolbert, "is that if the price agreed on at the beginning of the lease-purchase was $100,000 and the market value of the property goes up to $110,000, the renters still pay the agreed price of $100,000. The bank will see this almost as a refinance with equity already in the home. At the same time, if the market value of the home goes down, the renters can renegotiate or simply walk away and buy another home for less money."

Brian Fricke, a certified financial planner with Financial Management Concepts, in Winter Springs, Florida, says that typically, rent-to-own agreements can be negotiated for anywhere from one to three years. Sellers usually prefer a shorter contract since their ultimate goal is to sell the property.

"In this market, the renter would be likely to get three years if they want it," says Fricke. "That way, if you are unsure if the market has bottomed out, you can wait to see what happens."

Savitz says that when a lease/option arrangement works, with a solid buyer and a solid seller on either end of the deal, it can be beneficial to both sides.

"As long as you separate the rent money from the deposit money, this can help a young couple who's not quite ready to buy," says Savitz.

How Lease-Option Arrangements Work

No matter what the circumstances of a lease-option or lease-purchase arrangement, it's important for renters to consult with an attorney in order to protect their interests and to understand exactly what they are agreeing to do.

"I definitely recommend that buyers have an attorney look at any rent-to-own documents to make sure they are protected during the lease and at the end of the lease," says Fricke. "It's a very bad idea to rely on Internet-generated forms under these circumstances."

A rent-to-own contract should include the following arrangements to which both sides must agree:

- Specify the length of the lease period.

- Specify the amount of the monthly rent.

- Specify whether or not the sellers will be giving a credit to the renters toward a down payment, and, if so, how much and where it will be held for the renters to access at the time of purchase. Also, both sides need to agree about what will happen to the rent credit if the renters decide not to purchase at the end of the lease.

- Specify who will pay taxes, insurance, and homeowner/condominium association fees during the lease period (typically, the seller).

- Identify who will pay for utilities, maintenance, and repair during the lease period.

- Fricke says that typically a credit from the monthly rental payment is given back to the renter for a down payment, which usually justifies an above-market rent. The credit given is usually for that part of the rent that is above-market.

There are two ways to handle the transfer of title in a lease-to-own arrangement.

"Renters can start renting a place now and transfer the title later when they buy the place," says Tolbert. "An alternate arrangement is to arrange a contract for deed, which means that the title transfers immediately to the renters, and the owners are providing the financing."

Risks of Rent-to-Own Arrangements

Rent-to-own scenarios do carry some risks for renters and for sellers, which is why the services of an attorney are required when signing such agreements.

Holmgren says that usually in a lease-option arrangement the renters are paying a higher rent or making a larger deposit in the beginning of the lease than regular renters, which may not make the most sense financially.

Jancy Campbell, a broker associate with Real Estate of the Rockies, in Boulder, Colorado, says, "Rent-to-own arrangements can sometimes be a good option for a buyer, but they really need to compare the rent payments with a mortgage payment. Sellers who are giving a credit to the renters toward a down payment are usually charging above-market rent. The renters might be better off taking a less expensive rental and then saving up money for a down payment on their own."

Tolbert says she never arranges for a rent credit, although many rent-to-own arrangements include them.

"I don't believe in rent credits," says Tolbert. "The problem with them is that it is up to the loan underwriter when the renters apply for a loan to decide whether the rental payments can be considered part of the down payment. Many will count this ONLY if the credit is above the normal rent. The problem is that market-rate rents vary and can be hard to determine. The loan underwriter may not agree with the sellers on the market-rate rent for the property, and then the renters could lose the value of the money they thought would be applied to the down payment."

Tolbert recommends instead that people put $200 per month or whatever they wanted to be the rental credit aside in a separate savings account, which they won't access until the end of the lease.

In addition to rent credits, another major issue with a rent-to-own agreement is the title transfer.

"A big risk in a rent-to-own arrangement when the title isn't immediately transferred to the renters is that the property is affected by anything happening with the owner," says Tolbert. "For instance, a lien may be placed on the property, which can affect the title transfer later, or the owners may divorce and be in dispute over the property when the time comes to purchase it."

Ralph McMillan, a real estate attorney with McMillan-Terry, in Charlotte, North Carolina, says that sometimes in a lease-to-own arrangement the sale is considered to have taken place at the beginning of the lease. Consumers need to have a lawyer representing them and make sure the contract is negotiated to protect their interests and that they understand the consequences of taking title to the property.

Another important issue is home inspections.

"Buyers need to make sure that the home will be inspected when they buy the house, not when they move in, because the condition of the home could change," says McMillan.

While the renters are likely to carefully maintain a property they intend to buy, property can also be damaged by unforeseen circumstances such as a flood or fire, and systems and appliances age over time and may need repairs or replacement.

"It is very important to have it in writing whether the owners or renters are responsible for repairs," says McMillan. "Often, renters will take care of small things, but if the roof caves in, it better be in writing who has to fix it. These things need to be part of the negotiations for the lease-to-own agreement."

Whether the risks outweigh the benefits of a lease-to-own arrangement depends on the individual circumstances of potential buyers. For those with credit challenges or a lack of savings, this might be a viable option if structured appropriately. Buyers wary of buying a home that may drop in value can also use such an arrangement to their advantage while holding onto a property they like and watching the market for a year or so. But some legal experts believe the risks associated with rent-to-own deals are not worth the potential benefits.

Savitz says, "I hate lease-purchase arrangements because there are so many cautionary notes with them about ways things can go wrong. When the market gets tight, people try to bend the rules, but the bottom-line is that it is better to do things the right way. Lease-option arrangements can be dangerous, and there are just too many opportunities for either side to come out of them hurt. For instance, conceptually, part of the rent in these arrangements goes to a deposit on the purchase of the property, but if it is not structured correctly, any lender would treat this as an improper seller concession that won't be credited to the renter."

Bottom-line: this is one time where hiring an attorney, particularly one familiar with structuring a lease-to-buy arrangement, is a necessary expenditure.

✓ CHECKLIST

❑ If you have credit challenges or a lack of savings, look into the possibility of a lease-to-own agreement.

❑ If you are worried about home values dropping (or rising) in your area and want to wait out the market but find a home you would like to own, consider a one- or two-year lease-option arrangement.

❑ Consider the financial merits of simply renting while waiting out the market, improving your credit or building up your savings account.

❑ Hire an attorney before signing anything.

❑ Make sure if you enter a lease-to-own arrangement that every consideration is covered from rent credits to title transfer to home inspections to home maintenance and repairs.

Resources

iRentToOwn.com
Lease2Buy.com
MyRentToOwnHome.com
JSCinvestments.com
RentalHouses.com/rent-to-own
Reals.com/rent/rent-to-own
RentToOwnhomes.net

CHAPTER FOUR

Finding the Right, Reputable Realtor

When Joe moved to Seattle for a new job, he rented an apartment for a few months. As he settled into his job and his new hometown, he started looking up information about real estate on the Internet and realized that home prices were much more affordable than they were in northern New Jersey, where he had lived before. He visited an open house one Sunday at a condominium near his apartment and signed on with the real estate agent sitting at the house. Weeks later, Joe was receiving daily e-mails with dozens of possible townhomes and condominiums to look at, but he had no idea which neighborhood would be best for his lifestyle. He had not visited a lender, either, so he wasn't sure how much he could afford to spend. The real estate agent he was "working" with never returned his phone calls asking for advice, just kept e-mailing listings.

Why Your Realtor Matters

Like many inexperienced potential homebuyers, Joe neglected to take the necessary steps to find a Realtor who would provide the professional assistance needed to make the transition from renter to homeowner. Choosing the right real estate agent makes all the difference in the world to buyers, as well as sellers, particularly when a credit crisis could derail your financing at the last minute.

While first-time buyers may think the abundance of relatively affordable homes on the market means that buying property should be a snap, they should stop to think about the long-term consequences of buying the wrong home. For the vast majority of Americans, their home is the biggest long-term investment they will ever make. It just makes sense to have the expert advice of a real estate agent at this crucial time, someone to walk alongside the buyers to make sure they understand the contracts they are signing and the necessity of taking action and arranging for a home inspection, a termite inspection, homeowners insurance, title insurance, and more. Most people think a real estate agent exists to find property, but that is among the least important things a real estate agent does.

Since there are over 1.3 million Realtors across the country who are members of the National Association of Realtors (NAR), finding the right agent may seem daunting. But a real estate professional should be chosen in the same way that most people choose a doctor, a dentist, or a lawyer to work with: ask friends and colleagues to recommend someone. First-time buyers who have already been to see a lender for preapproval for a mortgage loan can also ask the lender for some names of reputable local real estate agents, since most lenders work directly with many agents.

Realtor or Real Estate Agent?

Throughout this book and most other written material about real estate, the terms "real estate agent" and "Realtor" are used pretty much interchangeably. But the truth is that those two terms are not the same, and the distinction that comes with the term "Realtor" is important.

David Kerr, a Realtor with ZipRealty, in San Francisco, says first-time buyers need to look for an agent who has the Realtor designation, which means that he is a member of the National Association of Realtors (NAR) and must adhere to the NAR Code of Ethics.

A real estate sales agent does not have to be a member of NAR, and anyone who is not a member does not have to follow the strict NAR Code of Ethics. NAR members must meet a number of additional requirements such as continuing education classes. NAR members face sanctions and penalties for violating the Code of Ethics. Realtors are also members of local Realtor associations, which are part of the series of checks-and-balances on agents and their conduct. An additional incentive for real estate agents to be ethical is a consistent need to work with other agents in each transaction. Realtors' reputations within a community are important to them and their ongoing business efforts.

Full-Time Agent or Part-Time?

In addition to choosing a NAR member as your Realtor representative, first-time buyers should make sure they work with a full-time agent, someone who can devote all their time to building their knowledge about homeowner programs, homes on the market, and neighborhoods.

"Buyers need to find an agent who is vested in the housing market as a full-time, experienced agent," says Angie Hicks, founder of Angie's List, a consumer group that provides members with information about local contractors and companies.

A part-time agent will likely hold another job, which distracts her from focusing on knowing everything about the changing real estate market. Some real estate agents have taken on part-time jobs to supplement their income during a slow housing market, but a reliable agent will stay focused full-time on selling homes, even if they need to work a second job.

Ask for Recommendations

Barbara Reynolds, president of marketing for Howard Hanna Realty Services, in Cleveland, Ohio, says, "First-time homebuyers should interview several agents and do the research on them. Don't just stop in and work with the first agent you meet. You need to connect with the agent emotionally and intellectually. A real estate transaction is a consulting sale, not a regular sale in which you have one meeting to buy or sell a product, so you really need to take the time to get referrals, check on testimonials from past clients, and check for information on the Internet about a potential agent."

Search by Neighborhood

If you know the area where you want to buy property, you can look up homes in that neighborhood or subdivision or condominium building online and look at the websites of agents that appear when searching. If you have visited a neighborhood you like and see several real estate signs from a particular agent, you can also go online to look at the websites of the agent and the real estate company to get a feel for what that agent may be like.

Kerr recommends that buyers ask what areas someone services to be sure they know the neighborhood well enough.

"Agents that work all over the place and in multiple states may not have the specific local expertise you need," he says. "Ask if they go on broker's tours and really know the local inventory. When a client registers on ZipRealty.com, they get assigned an agent who is an expert in the neighborhood where they are looking."

In this recessionary real estate market, Kerr says buyers should look online at sales statistics for different neighborhoods where they think they might want to live.

"When home prices are falling, buyers should look at current sales and narrow their focus onto neighborhoods that are doing okay, with relatively stable prices, and then find an agent in that area," Kerr says.

Hicks agrees that a local agent will understand the opportunities in an area and know whether you are getting a good deal or not according to the neighborhood.

Internet Resources

Many Realtors today write real estate blogs that can be accessed through their websites or by visiting ActiveRain.com and searching by name or location. A sister website to ActiveRain.com is Localism.com, which can provide local information including agent names, listings, and neighborhood information for consumers. Similar websites include CyberHomes.com and Trulia.com. The NAR website for finding agents and properties is Realtor.com.

Buyers can also check out reviews by other homebuyers and sellers of their real estate agents on a variety of websites, such as IncredibleAgents.com, AgentRank.com, or HomeGain.com. But just be sure to recognize that these sites often have only one or two reviews written about different agents, so you may only be reading about the experience of one very happy or very unhappy customer.

Working with a Team

The vast majority of Realtors work with both buyers and sellers at different times, but some specialize in working with only one of these groups. Others work in teams, with one or more agents working primarily with buyers and one or more working primarily with sellers. One question that first-time buyers should ask when they interview an agent who is part of a team is how much time that agent will spend with them. Some teams have large support staffs who contact clients, which could make the process less personal. On the other hand, teams do offer the advantage of having plenty of people available when you need questions answered. Many agents have a partner or an assistant who will be working directly with the buyer on some tasks. It really is a matter of personal preference and the comfort level of the buyers to decide whether to work with a team or an individual agent. If you are working with a team, make sure you are comfortable with each member you will be dealing with, especially the one with whom you will work most.

Representation and Buyer-Agent Agreements

Far more important than whether an agent is part of a team or not is to understand that your agent must represent your interests. Each agent represents either the buyer or the seller in a particular transaction. If you are buying a house, a condominium, or a townhouse, whether it's new or a resale, you need to have someone representing your interests from the very beginning. In many states, buyers are asked to sign a consent form, which simply states that the agent has disclosed that Realtors represent either the buyer or the seller in any transaction.

A buyer's agent will usually ask you to sign a buyer-agent agreement, which functions as a contract that should protect both the agent and the buyer. First-time buyers should be sure to read and understand the terms of the contract before signing. Signing a buyer-agent agreement does not mean that you must buy a specific house or even any house. It simply makes clear the rights and responsibilities of both the agent and the buyer.

The buyer promises to make sure the agent receives a commission for their services, generally paid out of the purchase price of the home by the seller. This means that the buyer essentially gets the services of the agent for free, since the commission comes from the profits of the sale of the home. Of course, the commissions paid to the buyer's agent and the seller's agent are considered when the seller agrees to a sales price during negotiations, since those fees will be paid from the seller's profits. But at least buyers do not have to come up with cash to pay the Realtor representing them at the settlement table or earlier in the home-purchase process.

In a buyer-agent contract, the agent promises to protect the buyer's interests throughout the transaction. Each state has different laws regarding real estate agents and how they represent their clients. Some companies exclusively represent only buyers so that there will never be a conflict of interest between the agents, buyer, and home sellers. Some agents work as exclusive buyer agents, never representing sellers under any circumstances. Most real estate offices have their agents work for either the buyer or the seller in any one transaction.

In regions where one real estate agency dominates the market, it's fairly common for the buyer and seller to be represented by agents who work for the same company, but this would not normally be a problem since agents operate as independent contractors. Rarely, an agent will act as a "dual agent," representing both the buyer and the seller. In a situation like this, it's extremely important to understand what information the agent will be sharing with the seller during negotiations and to acknowledge the potential conflict of interest for the agent.

Joseph Himali, principal broker of Best Address Real Estate, LLC, in Washington, D.C., says that consumers should be sure to understand the buyer-agent agreement before signing, focusing in particular on how to end the relationship if someone is unhappy.

"Often buyer or listing agreements require mutual written consent by the agent and the client to end the agreement, but I think the buyer or seller should be able to get out of the agreement at any time if they want to," says Mr. Himali. "The key for consumers and agents is that either party should have the ability to void the contract with twenty-four hours written notice."

Mr. Himali says that clients have two ways of making sure their agent serves them well.

"The carrot is the commission; the stick is the ability to cancel the contract," says Mr. Himali.

All terms in a buyer-agent agreement are negotiable, so buyers should ask for changes to anything they are uncomfortable signing.

Realtor Designations

Realtors often have a list of initials after their names, which represent designations they have achieved through continuing education classes beyond their initial real estate instruction and licensing exam. Some of the designations of interest to first-time homebuyers are listed at the end of this chapter. Each state has different requirements for Realtors to continue their education in order to maintain a license.

Diane Williams—an associate broker with Weichert Realtors, in their Spring House, Pennsylvania, office— recommends that first-time homebuyers work with a Realtor who is an Accredited Buyer Representative (ABR). This means the agent has taken a specific course for working with buyers, and they have more experience, which can be valuable to a first-time buyer.

Compatibility Counts

First-time buyers, particularly in a volatile real estate market, need to feel both confident of their Realtor's expertise and comfortable with them personally.

"A lot of buyers will call a listing agent for a property they are interested in, but then they don't know whether this agent is qualified or is a buyer agent," says Williams. "Buyers should meet two or three qualified agents and then decide which one will fit well with their personality. I'm a former nurse, which I think makes me more compassionate toward people and that can be helpful in this market when everyone is so nervous."

Some Realtors have a reputation for being extremely aggressive, actively searching for properties and pushing clients to make an offer on a home, which may be fine with some first-time buyers who are confident and ready to move forward. Other agents are more nurturing, taking the time to explain every step of the property buying process and making sure that the buyers are comfortable before going on to the next level.

Antoinette Matisoo, a broker/Realtor with Beacon Properties, in Holden, Massachusetts, says, "To find a good agent, you need to interview several agents either on the phone or in person and get a sense of their personality. There are expectations set on both the buyer side and the agent side, so you need to feel comfortable that the agent will meet your expectations. Agents should be asking you about your qualifications and begin educating you about the market."

Experienced Agent or Recently Trained?

Kerr suggests asking Realtors how long they have been in business.

"While it is good to have someone with experience, recognize that some agents who are new to the business will bust their asses for you even more than someone who has been around awhile," says Kerr.

Often new agents will consult extensively with another agent or the managing broker of their office, which can be a benefit to first-time buyers who need extra support. A potential hazard of working with an agent in business for decades is that they will have forgotten how complicated and scary the homebuying process is to a first-time buyer.

Questions to Ask

First-time buyers should ask a series of questions of potential agents in order to determine whether the Realtor has the right experience and a compatible personality. Hicks suggests asking about how many closings the agent handles each year and in what neighborhoods and price range. First-time buyers looking for an affordable home may not be well-served by an agent who usually handles high-end properties.

"Buyers who are concerned about a home holding onto its value and appreciating in years to come should ask a potential Realtor if she can provide some guidance as to what a home might need in terms of renovation and maintenance in the future," says Hicks. "An experienced agent will be able to help buyers recognize value in a property."

Jessie Brown, a Realtor with Weichert Realtors, in Charlotte, North Carolina, says buyers need to find an agent who is knowledgeable about the area but also someone who cares about them.

Brown says, "Buyers should ask: 'Can you help me get approved for a loan? Do you know a lot of reliable lenders? Do you know about all types of financing options? What about first-time buyer programs, FHA loans, VA loans? Can you match my circumstances with your experience? Will you manage the whole process? Help me find a home inspector and get through settlement? Will you be able to help me figure out whether something is a good deal?'"

Researching References

Reynolds says that in addition to connecting emotionally and intellectually with a potential buyer's agent, first-time homebuyers should do some research on the agent to make sure they have the information and integrity needed to be a strong representative of the buyer's interests.

"You really need to take the time to get referrals, check on testimonials from past clients, and check for information on the Internet about a potential agent," says Reynolds.

Agents should be asked for a list of references, and the consumers should follow up by calling these references to ask about their experience with the Realtor. Real estate agents can also be investigated by looking them up on Google.com and Facebook.com.

Consumers should also check their state real estate commissions to determine whether an agent has the required active real estate license and whether any complaints have been filed against him or her. Each state has a slightly different way of searching for credentials, but usually this takes a matter of minutes. Those minutes could be crucial if you find you are about to hire a real estate agent with a string of past complaints against her. (A list of these commissions can be found in the appendix.)

The First Buyer-Agent Meeting

Reynolds says that in addition to answering questions from the buyers, a good Realtor will educate the buyer step-by-step throughout the process and present a sample contract at the first meeting.

Matisoo says she spends an hour or more at the very first appointment going over the contract and making sure the buyers understand every part of it before they even look at houses.

Williams says her initial meeting with a potential buyer includes the following steps, which serve as an example of what a first-time buyer should expect from a meeting with a Realtor. She suggests including anyone who might be part of the decision-making process at the initial meeting. Many first-time buyers, especially if they are single, choose a parent, sibling, or trusted friend to be their "second pair of eyes" when making such an important investment. This person should be part of the process from the beginning, including choosing a Realtor.

Williams says the first buyer-Realtor meeting should last about one hour and cover the following:

Preapproval

If you have a preapproval letter from a reputable lender, you should bring it to the meeting. If not, you and your agent should discuss the need for preapproval before launching a serious home search. Another option at this first meeting is for the agent, with your permission, to arrange for a reputable mortgage lender to attend part of the meeting to review and begin the preapproval process. Also, this lender can give you a general idea as to what you can afford and what the closing costs will be. You are under no obligation to use this lender for your mortgage; this is meant to give you an idea of what you can afford.

The Importance of a Quality Lender

At some point during the agent and buyer meeting, the agent should discuss why it's imperative that you have a reputable lender. If your lender has not been recommended by a friend or relative, it's appropriate for you to ask for references from the lender. Realtors have had nightmare experiences with lenders who are not able to proceed to settlement because the promised funding or programs (including interest rates) are no longer available. Likewise, buyers can have their dreams and plans crushed by financing that falls through at the last minute.

Agency Services and Conflicts

The agent should go over the buyer-agent agreement with you and explain the importance of understanding which agent is representing which person in any transaction. Most agents prepare a folder for the buyer with printed information about what to expect during the whole buying process, with sample contracts and forms, folders about home warranty programs, and contact information for insurance, utility, and moving companies. This folder should be expected at the initial meeting. If you don't receive any printed information, ask the agent for sample documents and contact information or any other items that you think might be helpful.

Needs and Wants

Discuss your time frame for moving and other wants and needs, including location, lot size, age of the home, number of bedrooms and baths, basement, garage, family room, fireplace, etc. This is the time to emphasize your priorities and to make sure the agent understands them. A good agent can help you refine your priorities and think about some aspects of a home that you might not have considered, such as whether you prefer a kitchen in the front of the house or the back, or an open floor plan or a more formal one.

The Process

Your potential agent should review in general the "buying process" from the beginning until settlement, including such important steps as signing the agreement of sale, the mortgage application, insurance needed, and all the inspections. You should ask as many questions as you can during this part of the meeting because the more you understand now the better your whole experience will be.

Searches and Contact

Your agent should demonstrate a "prospect" search in the MLS (Multiple Listing Service) on the computer. You and the agent should decide how often to be in contact and whether you prefer e-mail, phone calls, or text messages. You can decide if you want to receive e-mails on prospective properties daily, twice a week, weekly, or as soon as the properties become available.

Viewings

Discuss the plan for visiting properties. You may want to start out looking at properties online, then drive by the home, and if you are still interested, call your Realtor to make an appointment to visit it. You and your agent should talk about how many properties your agent is willing to show and how often. What are your expectations? What are your agent's expectations? If you are buying with someone else, talk about whether you both need to be at every viewing. Ask your agent what the rules are about you visiting open houses or model homes at new developments. Generally, once you have signed an agreement and committed to working with an agent, you can still look at homes on your own and bring in your agent when you are ready to make an offer on a property, whether it is a new home or a resale.

Agreement-of-Sale Process

Your agent should discuss the "agreement-of-sale" process and present a list of recent comparable homes sold in targeted neighborhoods so you can start gauging realistic offers. You and your agent should talk about potential negotiation tactics. For example, your potential Realtor should tell you that part of the negotiating process is knowing how long a property has been on the market, what the original asking price was, and getting a feel for the urgency of the seller. If the settlement date is extremely important to the seller, then there is a possibility they would accept a lower price if they can close on that date. Remember that terms are often as important as price.

Other Issues

Your agent should discuss other issues that might affect the purchase or resale of a property: the importance of checking out school districts, the overall desirability of a neighborhood, why it's good not to be the highest-priced home in a neighborhood, busy roads, future planned roads or developments, anything you might want to know. For example, is there a toxic waste dump nearby or plans to tear down a forest to build a parking garage? Your agent should talk with you about whether the neighborhood is changing for better or for worse. First-time buyers often don't have the foresight or experience to consider these things, but they need to ask questions and do as much research as they can on their own.

In fact, under the rules of the Fair Housing Act, agents need to be careful not to violate standards of fairness and may instead simply tell buyers where they can find that kind of information on their own. (See more on this topic in the next chapter, "Location, Location . . . Choosing the Right Neighborhood.)

Local government websites and real estate information sites offer information about neighborhoods and planned developments, and real estate agents are required to share their knowledge about things such as which areas are subject to flooding and where roads may be built. The Fair Housing Act rules apply to subjective opinions such as labeling a school or a neighborhood as "good" or "bad" or "the best."

To Sign or Not to Sign

At the end of the meeting, your agent should review the buyer-agent agreement again. If you don't feel ready to sign it and would rather read it over and think about it, ask if you can take it home. Some agents insist that you sign an agreement before beginning to show you properties, but others will begin this process even without a signed agreement.

Clearly, the initial meeting with a Realtor should provide detailed information for you along with a sense of personal compatibility between the buyers and the agent. Buyers who feel uncomfortable with an agent or find it difficult to ask her questions should continue interviewing agents until they find someone who is easier to communicate with.

✓ CHECKLIST

Questions to Ask Your Potential Realtor:

❑ Are you a Realtor? (A member of the National Association of Realtors)

❑ Do you work full-time as a Realtor?

❑ Are you an Accredited Buyers' Representative (ABR)?

❑ Are you experienced working with first-time homebuyers?

❑ Can you tell me about state, local, and federal programs for first-time homebuyers?

❑ Can you help me qualify for a mortgage or direct me to a lender who can help me?

❑ What neighborhoods do you specialize in?

❑ What price range do you usually work in?

❑ Can you provide me with a list of references I can contact?

❑ What is the fastest way for me to reach you if I have a question or think I have found a place to buy?

❑ How often should I expect to hear from you while I am looking for a home?

❑ Will you be able to give me advice about future home maintenance or improvement projects that will help my house retain its value?

Resources for Realtor Reviews:

- IncredibleAgents.com

- AgentRank.com

- HomeGain.com

Realtor Designations:

- ABR: Accredited Buyer Representative (passed coursework focused on working with buyers).

- CRS: Certified Residential Specialist (awarded to experienced Realtors who have completed advanced training and have extensive selling and listing experience).

- GRI: Graduate, Realtor Institute (higher level of solid education in all aspects of real estate).

- e-PRO: (a designation earned entirely online to certify agents as Internet professionals).

- Green Designation: (earned by real estate professionals with training in residential markets and environmentally friendly practices).

CHAPTER FIVE

Location, Location . . . Choosing the Right Neighborhood

Weichert Realtor Jessie Brown recently worked with a first-time buyer determined to spend only her maximum budget of $49,950 for a home in Charlotte, North Carolina. She and Brown searched for months, rejecting homes that needed too many repairs, then found a home she thought she wanted which was in good condition. But Brown referred her to the crime reports for Charlotte, where she discovered that this supposedly desirable home was located in a high crime area. She realized it was not worth it to her to live in a nice home but not have any peace of mind. She and Brown agreed that the home was unlikely to appreciate in value, either, since it was located in a neighborhood where few people wanted to live. Brown continued to search for homes with this client until they were able to find one she could both feel safe in and afford.

Choosing a neighborhood is a crucial part of buying a home, one that some homebuyers ignore in favor of house hunting. Buyers relocating to an unfamiliar area have a particularly tough job narrowing down their home search since all neighborhoods look the same on a street map. But even buyers looking in their hometown may have trouble recognizing what makes a neighborhood desirable and what will therefore help the homes there maintain their value.

As the housing market slumped, Realtors tracking home prices recognized more vividly than ever the importance of a neighborhood. As some areas watched their home values plummet by double-digit percentages, individual neighborhoods within these areas had homes drop in value only slightly or maintain their value. A few even saw home prices increase while the rest of their state struggled with mounting foreclosures and homeowners "underwater," owing more than their home was worth. For example, in Arlington, Virginia, many homes increased in estimated value by 1 or 2% in 2008, while in Manassas, only about twenty miles away, home values in some communities plunged by 40% that year.

Potential homebuyers and their agents should examine a wide variety of factors when narrowing down their choice of neighborhoods. Under the rules of the Fair Housing Act, Realtors are not allowed to recommend specific neighborhoods or school districts to their customers because of the concern that buyers would be "steered" to neighborhoods along racial, religious, or ethnic lines. When potential buyers ask Realtors about specific demographic information such as crime statistics or school test scores, real estate agents are allowed to direct their clients to places where they can easily obtain that information.

Clearly, most choices are extremely individual. For instance, while one family prefers to live in a planned community with similar homes and rules that ensure that the properties are maintained, another family would rather live in a neighborhood where the homeowners are free to paint their homes any color they want and grow vegetables in their front yard instead of a lawn. Some buyers want to live in a contemporary-style condominium building with a fitness center, coffee bar, and party room on the premises, while others prefer a one-hundred-year-old home in an area with protective covenants to preserve the historic architecture of the neighborhood.

But some factors make any neighborhood preferable to others, such as a low crime rate and good schools. Potential homeowners without children may think the school district is unimportant; but in terms of the eventual resale value of the home, a school district with a good reputation will always be more desirable for most homebuyers than one with a poor reputation.

The Economy and Neighborhood Values

Marty Frame, general manager of CyberHomes.com, says, "A fundamental determining factor in real estate values is employment. For instance, in California right now, we have a bad real estate market, but good employment. This bodes well for the future of California real estate, unlike Florida or Nevada, where the real estate became overpriced and job growth is flat. Empirical signs of good employment can mean that a location may be a good place to buy. Up until the stock market started being so badly hurt, the New York City market was not affected by the housing crisis. But now that the financial industry is seeing layoffs and their bonuses are being cut, housing prices are falling there, too."

Job growth for different cities and communities can be tracked by searching online at web sites such as Fortune.com, which regularly lists cities and states that are experiencing job and population growth.

Tracking Home Prices

In addition to checking on job growth, home values can easily be tracked, especially by real estate agents with access to their local multiple listing service (MLS).

"To make sure a place will hold its value, buyers should look at what sold in an area and how close the sale price was to the assessed value," says Antoinette Matisoo, a broker/Realtor from Holden, Massachusetts. "The biggest thing buyers are afraid of is a home dropping in value, but we are starting to see some consistent history in some parts of the country so comparisons can be made."

Websites, such as CyberHomes.com, allow consumers to track market dynamics on their own.

Frame says, "The numbers on CyberHomes.com let home-owners or potential buyers look at how stable or volatile prices are along with what is driving those prices. You can look at historical resiliency in a neighborhood, in other words, areas where in this recent down market home prices have stayed stable or not dropped as much. In many areas of the country, this means the closer to downtown you are, the more stable the housing values are."

David Kerr, a Realtor with ZipRealty, in San Francisco, says there are micromarkets even within individual zip codes that have held their own better than others, so that's why it's important to look at that price history.

Barbara Reynolds, president of marketing for Howard Hanna Realty Services, in Cleveland, Ohio, says, "In our area, prices seem to be leveling off, so there's a 99% probability that the homes will eventually increase in value. Buyers need to see the real data so that they can understand where prices have been and where they might go."

Internet Tools

In addition to tracking home prices, a variety of Internet sites can provide other statistical and anecdotal information about individual neighborhoods. On websites such as CyberHomes.com, Localism.com, and Trulia.com, you can find out information such as how many people speak French in a certain neighborhood, what the average level of education is, and the average age of the local residents.

"Look for a neighborhood that looks like you," says Frame. "For instance, if you want to live in an area popular with academic types or military families, you can search for demographics like that online."

Another web site, WalkScore.com, measures the "walkability" of individual locations, measuring how far it is to walk to public transportation, grocery stores, libraries, and other conveniences. The ZipRealty website (ZipRealty.com) also features this information.

Kerr says that once potential buyers have identified a neighborhood on the Internet that looks interesting, they should drive around the neighborhood to see if it appeals to them, especially during the times of day when they are likely to be home.

"If a neighborhood is inexpensive but not convenient for you, then it doesn't make sense to buy there," says Kerr. "Sometimes it is worth stretching your budget to get into a good area."

Location

Most homebuyers start by looking at neighborhoods that are convenient to their work either by a short drive or easily accessible public transportation. But it's important to recognize the potential for a job change in the future, especially for households with two working members. An appealing location should be one that's convenient to a wide range of amenities, transportation options, and employment centers so that it functions well for more than one family member and for potential future buyers.

"Almost no matter where you are in the country, neighborhoods with good schools tend to hold their value better than others, along with neighborhoods with close proximity to shopping centers and public transportation and good commuter routes," says Kerr. "The outlying areas with long commutes are the ones that have lost the most value in this current housing market, especially when gas prices shot up."

Reputation: The Three Top Determining Factors

Neighborhoods, whether convenient or not, often have a reputation as straightforward as "good" or "bad." When most people make judgments on a community, they will consider the schools, the crime rate, and the appearance of the homes in the area.

Andy Tolbert, a Realtor with HD Realty, in the Orlando, Florida area, says, "Buyers should look for neighborhoods where people *want* to live, not where they *have* to live. Talk to people everywhere about different areas, especially if you are new to a city, to get a feel for what places are popular and why."

Frame says that school districts are important regardless of whether the buyers have kids or intend to have kids, since they make a neighborhood more attractive to potential buyers. "Even undervalued homes in great school districts will be a better long-term investment than an overvalued home in a bad school district," says Frame.

Tolbert says that doing the research to find out which schools are highly rated is crucial for buyers concerned about the future value of their home. "If you are in a family-oriented neighborhood with bad schools it will be hard to sell," says Tolbert.

Crime statistics are important to everyone, whether they are buying a home or renting and whether they have children or not. No one wants to live in a neighborhood with high crime. Unfortunately low home prices do not always correlate with low crime, so many people make compromises in order to afford a home. Buyers can contact the local police station to ask for crime reports on specific neighborhoods or visit

CrimeReports.com to search by an address or a zip code for recent crime information.

Of course, crime statistics do not necessarily mean that a majority of the residents in a particular neighborhood are crime victims. Many entrepreneurial homebuyers opt to live in a neighborhood on the edge of a high-crime area or a community that is in the process of revitalization because the property values should rise as the area improves. The danger of buying in this type of neighborhood, in addition to the chance of becoming a crime victim, is that conditions won't improve, and the home will be difficult to sell. Evaluating that risk is part of the process of choosing a home.

"Bad" neighborhoods are sometimes identified as such simply because of the appearance of the homes. If the homes all have iron bars on the ground floor windows and five or more locks on the front door, then the assumption is that this is not a safe neighborhood.

But even communities that aren't "bad" can be evaluated based on appearance. Neighborhoods where the lawns are mowed, weeds are pulled, the trash is picked up, and window frames are kept painted are naturally more appealing and can be an indicator of a continually appealing community.

"It's important to look for areas with pride of ownership, because those are communities which are more likely to hold onto their value," says Frame.

Homeowners Associations

Neighborhoods with a homeowners association (HOA) usually have the advantage of an appealing appearance since the association rules usually require at least a minimal requirement of maintaining the exterior of a property. Some planned communities require that homes have the same front light fixtures and may only be painted within the color scheme of the development, while others are looser and simply require that lawns are kept mowed and that the homes don't have any peeling paint.

HOA dues vary widely from community to community, with some including recreational amenities such as swimming pools and tennis courts and clubhouses with fitness facilities and party rooms, while others only cover trash and snow removal for the neighborhood streets. A few include lawn and landscaping care even for the individual homes. Potential buyers need to be very aware of what the additional costs of HOA will add to their housing expenses and what the fees pay for, because if they want to take advantage of neighborhood amenities that are not included in the fee, such as a swimming pool, they will need to budget for those expenses, too. Nonpayment of HOA fees will eventually result in a lien against the home, which will make it impossible to refinance or sell until the fees are repaid.

In some areas, virtually all new homes are part of a community with an HOA, so buyers looking for a new home have little choice but to belong to an HOA.

Brown says, "A lot of people prefer to stay out of a community with a homeowners association because they want to avoid restrictions and extra payments. But in our area of North Carolina, almost everything built after 2000 is in an HOA."

Brown points out that—on the positive side—HOA rules do help protect the value of the house since the homes are usually well maintained.

"It's really important for buyers to study the guidelines and covenants of an HOA before buying to make sure they live with the restrictions," says Brown. "For instance, a family that plans to offer daycare services in their home should check to be sure this is allowed under the HOA rules. Some communities don't allow it. Others won't allow boats or RVs to be parked in the community, so buyers who own them really need to check to see if they can bring them into the neighborhood."

Pick-up trucks and commercial vehicles are also banned from being parked in some communities. (See also Chapter Ten: Legal and Tax Implications of Homebuying)

Consider Potential Development

In addition to thinking about the benefits and drawbacks to living in a community with a homeowners association, buyers need to be aware of the setting of a neighborhood within an area with an eye to future development. Buyers can ask their Realtors for information about planned developments and can research on their own through the local planning and zoning office. This is less important for buyers moving into an area that is established and has little room for new roads or shopping centers, but even within cities, plans are made for tearing down buildings and adding new ones. Buyers need to be aware of plans that could affect their quality of life and the future value of their home. A home that backs to a peaceful patch of woods will not be so appealing when it backs to a three-lane highway in a few years.

Diane Williams, an associate broker with Weichert Realtors, in Springhouse, Pennsylvania, says, "You don't want to buy a house on a busy road or backing up to a turnpike. Buyers in new areas need to really carefully look at the location and future plans for development in the area. You also want to own a place not too far from major roads and your workplace."

Tolbert suggests that in addition to moving close to shopping areas and public transportation, buyers should keep thinking about how the neighborhood will appeal to other buyers in the future.

"Your home may even turn into a rental unit for you someday, so keep the guidelines in mind of what renters might be looking for," says Tolbert.

Matching Your Money with the Right Neighborhood

While buyers may identify their first-choice neighborhood, they may not always be able to find a home they can afford there.

"First-time buyers are generally not able to buy right into a prime neighborhood, but they want to be near it, to walk or to drive to a prime neighborhood," says Frame. "They may need to compromise to be near or in a prime neighborhood with the size of the home or maybe living on a busy street in order to afford to buy, but it is worth it if you can be in a desirable area."

Part of the process of searching for a home is determining your priorities and matching them with a home that will be likely to hold onto its value over time. Most homebuyers, especially first-time buyers, have to make compromises in order to buy a home.

Matisoo says, "I was working with a young couple that was looking for a home in a particular neighborhood, but they really couldn't afford a place with everything they wanted in that area. Once I got a sense of what they were looking for, I started to comb the Internet for homes that had everything they wanted in nearby neighborhoods. They ended up buying a great house in a great location that was more affordable for them."

In addition to finding a desirable neighborhood, buyers should think about how the home they are interested in purchasing fits into that neighborhood.

"You don't want to own the most expensive house in the neighborhood. This brings the value of your house down, not up," says Williams.

Kerr goes farther than that, recommending to his clients that they should always buy the worst house in the best neighborhood because it is sure to go up in value.

Calculating which neighborhood is the most desirable and which home is the right one within that neighborhood is a daunting task that carries with it the risk of a miscalculation.

But Williams has some advice for buyers that should be a comfort to those who are wary of making a bad investment.

"Remember that this is not just an investment, but a refuge. You are buying a hearth and home," says Williams.

✓ CHECKLIST

❏ Ask your Realtor to track pricing to identify neighborhoods that have historically held their value in different housing markets.

❏ Use Internet search sites to gather information about demographics and locations of amenities within different neighborhoods.

❏ Review crime statistics to make sure you are buying into a safe neighborhood.

❏ Review school reports even if you don't have children because homes in good school districts historically hold their value.

❏ Find a neighborhood near a variety of transportation options for easier commuting.

❏ Decide if you want to live in a community with a homeowners association.

❏ Drive or walk through the neighborhood to see the condition of the homes and streets.

❏ Look at the neighborhood at the times of day when you are likely to be home to see if you will be comfortable there.

❏ Don't buy the most expensive home in the neighborhood, the value is not likely to increase.

❏ Research potential future area developments that could affect the value of your home.

Frame's Five Simple Steps to Finding the Right Neighborhood

1. **Rush-hour roulette.** Many people include commute time to work when considering important quality of life indicators. If you know spending more than thirty minutes to and from work is too long in the car (or on the train), then look for a neighborhood first that offers a manageable commute for all working adults in the household. Not only will you save money on gas, you will get to spend more time in your new home.

2. **Know thy neighbor.** Decide what type of neighborhood most suits you and then do some research. Sites like CyberHomes.com can give you information on the makeup of a neighborhood, including information on population and overhead maps. If you are looking for a very quiet community with no neighbors in sight, be sure you aren't checking out a neighborhood where houses share a fence in the backyard.

3. **Get schooled on local education.** If you're a family, finding a neighborhood in a quality school district is high on the priority list. Don't just rely on individuals to find out what schools are the best, as what's important can differ greatly from one parent to another. There are a variety of good online resources that offer school comparisons for districts and cities across the country, such as SchoolMatch.com.

4. **How far is it to the closest grocery store?** Find out how accessible local amenities are to the neighborhood, including grocery stores, movie theaters, and restaurants. If you want to live in a populated neighborhood, you are looking in the wrong place if the closest store is more than ten miles away. Sites like "Yahoo! Maps" (Maps.Yahoo.com) allow you to look up an address and map the commercial amenities around it.

5. **Do a walk through.** Once you have identified a potential neighborhood through initial research, visit the neighborhood on a Saturday afternoon. A weekend visit gives you the best chance to see the most people out of their homes, and you can get a pulse on the energy (or lack thereof!) of the neighborhood. Walk around, talk to residents and have specific questions ready.

Resources

- Localism.com
- CrimeReports.com
- CyberHomes.com
- Zillow.com
- Trulia.com
- Realtor.com
- RealEstate.Yahoo.com/neighborhoods
- YourStreet.com
- RealEstate.aol.com/neighborhood-index
- SchoolMatch.com
- WalkScore.com

CHAPTER SIX

Narrowing Your Property Choice

When Karen and George decided they wanted to take advantage of low interest rates and falling home prices, they were concerned most about staying within their budget. Their lender told them they could afford a $400,000 mortgage. A fixed-rate loan with an interest rate of 5.25% meant that their payments would be about $2,200 per month for just principal and interest. But the couple's rent was only $1,500 per month, and they really did not want to spend a lot more than that. They decided to stick to a mortgage loan maximum of $300,000, which at that same rate, carried monthly payments of $1,656.

With only a little over $10,000 available for a down payment, the couple needed to a find a home priced under $315,000. After weeks of searching with their Realtor for a home, they chose a foreclosure in a neighborhood they liked. Focused entirely on price, the couple did not consider two important factors that should have influenced their choice: satisfying their preferences and contemplating their investment in terms of resale value.

While the home they bought fit into their budget, it had only one bathroom. After they moved in, they realized that the cost of adding a second bathroom far exceeded their expectations and their budget. In addition, within two blocks of their newly purchased home, there were ten homes that had undergone foreclosure and were in the process of being sold at an even deeper discount. It would be years before their home and the others in the community would recoup their former value and increase above what Karen and George paid for it.

Balancing Emotion and Financial Sense

While Karen and George are admirable for their adherence to their budget, they neglected to go the extra step to make sure that what they were buying was worth the price they paid and would have a positive investment potential.

Marty Frame, general manager of CyberHomes.com, says, "Buying a home is very emotional and an intimidating process. First, stick to the data and that will help overcome the emotion. First-time buyers should be especially careful to work with a Realtor to analyze the sales and price statistics on a property and a neighborhood when they find a home they think they want to buy."

Frame says that evaluating the pattern of values in a neighborhood can function as a predictor of future value, which should be a consideration when narrowing your choice of property.

"Smart buyers know: if you can't afford the biggest house in the best location, then you should go for the smallest house in the best location," says Frame.

While Karen and George followed the advice of choosing a small home, they neglected to evaluate the impact of the cluster of foreclosures on the neighborhood. In this economy, it is rare to find a neighborhood without a property that has undergone foreclosure. But there is a big difference between a neighborhood with one or two foreclosures versus one with ten or more within a couple of blocks. Neighborhoods with a significant number of foreclosures will take far longer to increase in value than those with just a few, since appraisers rely on comparable sales to establish home values. If half the houses in a community have been foreclosed on and sold at 75% or less of the market value, this could significantly impact the market value of all the homes in the neighborhood for a long time to come.

In addition to paying attention to foreclosures, there are certain elements that help a home hold onto its value. These elements vary from area to area across the country. For instance, East Coast single-family homes are considered more desirable if they have a basement, particularly if it has been finished. But in other parts of the country, basements are essentially nonexistent. In South Florida, a swimming pool adds value to a home, while in many Northern parts of the country a swimming pool is looked at as an expensive liability.

Andy Tolbert, a Realtor with HD Realty, in the Orlando, Florida area, says that certain elements in a home will consistently help a home hold onto its value no matter where it is located.

"Always buy a home with at least two baths, otherwise it will be almost impossible to sell," says Tolbert. "A home with at least three bedrooms and two baths will always eventually find a buyer no matter what the market is like."

If you are buying a home in a subdivision where most homes have four bedrooms and three and one-half baths, you should probably avoid buying a home with three bedrooms and two baths, though, because it will be less appealing to families looking at other residences in the community.

Buyers always need to match their emotional desire for a home while understanding the implications of such a major investment. In this current climate where many homeowners have gotten over their heads by spending too much on a house or have lost their jobs due to the recession, more homes are available at lower prices than usual, especially if the owners are in the process of foreclosure or the lender has already taken possession of the home. But first-time buyers should be wary of snapping up a home just because it seems like a good value. Long-term value depends on much more than the initial purchase price.

Keep Resale Potential in Mind

While the last thing many buyers want to consider when they are choosing a home is selling it, the savvy buyer always gives a little bit of thought to the future. Of course, it's impossible to know for certain when you might want to sell your house or what the housing market will be like at that point, but some universal truths still hold when it comes to houses.

Tolbert says, "Always look at every property for potential resale value. For instance if you fall in love with a really odd house, know that when you try to sell, it will be much harder to find someone else to buy a unique or unusual property."

That doesn't mean you shouldn't buy it, but you should be aware that you may need to give yourself more time when you sell it. You may find that this is a property that increases in value not at all or very slowly.

Diane Williams, an associate broker with Weichert Realtors, in Springhouse, Pennsylvania, says that at the very first meeting with new buyers, she discusses their preferences for a home.

"Often, they don't even really know what they want, or the husband and wife don't realize that they don't agree on everything until they start to talk about it," says Williams. "For instance, they need to talk about whether they want an older home or a new one, how big a lot they want and every other detail such as fireplaces and how many bedrooms they need."

Even if buyers opt for an older home, they should consider how many home improvements have been done to a home. While older homes can be charming, buyers should understand that if the windows and the roof have never been replaced, these could be major projects (and expensive ones) that might be necessary to undertake within a few years.

Sometimes first-time buyers can be dazzled by all the amenities in a home or the sheer size of a home compared to a rental apartment, but they need to stop and consider some mundane aspects of homeownership such as making sure the furnace works and the water heater is in good repair. A home inspection can provide valuable information about the life expectancy of systems and appliances, as well as an estimate of the cost of replacing or repairing these items.

While it's important to narrow priorities and preferences in a home, Williams also says buyers need to think about their time frame for buying.

"Some buyers know they need to move within a month or so because their lease is up, but others aren't ready to move for eight or nine months," says Williams. "This should be part of the discussion and will affect what you look at."

Some potential buyers have spent so much time thinking about buying a home or even looking at properties online or in person that they have a very clear idea of what they want to own. A Realtor can put their ideas into perspective along with what they can afford and what might be likely to hold onto its value in the long-term.

Realtor Jessie L. Brown, with Weichert Realtors, in Charlotte, North Carolina, says, "After prequalifying someone to make sure they know what they can afford, we sit down and discuss what they want to buy. Some people have to have a certain number of bedrooms and baths, others want a first-floor master suite. Then we narrow down the list through an Internet search and start visiting the houses four or five at a time. Over a few months, some people will look at twenty or thirty places. By the time they are done with that, they usually know what they want."

In some cases, though, the buyers involve other family members or friends in the final decision on which property to buy. Making that final leap into making an offer can be extremely frightening, particularly in uncertain economic times. But buyers should make sure they are accepting advice from knowledgeable friends or family members. If these advisors are to have a significant voice in the choice of property, then the potential buyers should consider including them throughout the buying process rather than after a property of choice has been identified.

Williams, when working with a young couple who wanted to buy their first home, followed the prescribed steps of getting them prequalified for a mortgage and determining their price range, identifying a neighborhood that fit their budget and their lifestyle, and then narrowing their priorities. She helped the couple find a townhouse they loved, and they were ready to make an offer. At that point, the couple brought their out-of-town parents who were helping them with the down payment, to visit the house. The two sets of parents, none of whom had bought a house in more than twenty years, reacted to the house this couple found so charming by saying, "You're going to buy *that* house for *that* much money?"

The couple decided not to make an offer and continued searching, but every place they saw they compared to the one they had passed up. Eventually they purchased a place that satisfied their parents, but not one they loved as much as their first choice.

This young couple seemed to be taking all the right steps to purchase their first home in these trying times, including preparing themselves financially for what is likely to be the biggest investment they will ever make. But one important step was skipped: they did not include everyone who would be part of the decision-making process from the beginning. If this couple intended to have their parents assist them with the purchase and agreed that they could have a say in the choice of home, they should have included them during the initial period of comparing what they could afford with the available homes in their area so that they would have a greater understanding of the local market.

Picking just the right house to fit into your budget, satisfy your preference, and provide the potential to increase in value can be daunting. But buyers who prepare themselves with financial knowledge and the advice of a local market expert are more likely to make an intelligent choice than someone who buys purely on the basis of emotion.

✓ **CHECKLIST**

❑ Consider the potential future resale value of a home when you're narrowing your choices. While future markets are nearly impossible to predict, some elements (such as having at least two bathrooms) will always help a home keep its value. Keeping to your budget is crucial in this economy, but you also don't want to buy a house that will lose value over time.

❑ Make sure you a buy a home that fits in with the preferences of other homebuyers in your area, such as a basement or a swimming pool or the number of bathrooms and bedrooms.

❑ Check to see if the homes in the area where you want to buy include a lot of foreclosures, which could negatively impact the home values in the area for a long time.

CHAPTER SEVEN

Short Sales, Foreclosures, and Auctions

When Julie and Paul became engaged, they agreed that they wanted to buy a home that would be ready for move-in when they returned from their honeymoon. They searched for homes near their offices in Fairfax, Virginia, and were amazed to find more homes than they expected that fit their budget of $450,000. Instead of starting homeownership by buying a two-level townhome as they had anticipated, the Rodgers found a charming, nearly new single-family home in their price range. The home was listed as a "short sale," a term they had never heard.

Julie and Paul's real estate agent told them that a short sale just meant that the sellers' lender would need to accept their offer for the home along with the sellers. She neglected to explain that in many cases, approval of a short sale can take two or three months or longer because lenders have a backlog of mortgages in default to handle. The couple's wedding day came and went without an acceptance of their offer by the sellers' lender. Weeks after their honeymoon, as they packed their apartment in anticipation of moving into their new home, the lender turned down their offer. Julie and Paul started their home search all over again, vowing to avoid any type of home purchase other than a standard buyer-seller transaction. Happily, they were able to

find another single family home they found appealing, which, while
smaller than their first choice, they were able to purchase and move
into within thirty days.

Barbara Reynolds, president of marketing for Howard Hanna
Realty Services, in Cleveland, Ohio says, "First-time buyers can
look at foreclosures and short sales, but they need to be very
sure that they are working with a Realtor who has experience
with foreclosures and can educate them about how these sales
are different from regular home purchases. Buying a
foreclosure can be complicated, so buyers need to be patient
and make sure they understand the process."

Angie Hicks, founder of Angie's List, a consumer group that
provides members with information about local contractors
and companies, says that buyers interested in purchasing a
foreclosure or a short sale should be sure to work with an
agent who knows the neighborhood well, so she can make a
good evaluation of the worth of the property in comparison
with other homes.

"Make sure you can do an inspection on the property and
are prepared to handle the necessary repairs and, most
important, make sure you're not getting into a money pit,"
says Hicks.

Short Sales

The first thing buyers need to understand is the difference
between buying a foreclosure and a short sale.

A foreclosure, also known as an "REO or Real Estate
Owned" by the bank, is a home that has been repossessed and
is now under the ownership of the bank. Since banks and
other financial institutions prefer not to hold onto property,
they offer these foreclosed-on homes for sale, often at below-
market prices.

A short sale, when the owners place the property on the market themselves, is an effort to prevent a foreclosure. A short sale requires an agreement between the homeowners and their mortgage holder in which the lender agrees to accept an offer for the home that is less than the full amount owed on the property. Short sales may look like a great deal for the buyers, who can snap up a property at a lower price, but there are a number of risks associated with purchasing a short sale.

"Lots of first-time buyers will be discouraged if they try to buy a short sale because they are excited at first and then get frustrated by the length of time involved," says Tolbert.

A short sale can take sixty to ninety days or longer to reach settlement and buyers need to be ready for their offer to be turned down by the bank even after waiting all that time.

"Short sales are not necessarily a bargain, either, because lenders need the home to sell at a price close to the current market value," says Tolbert. "That said, in some areas of the country you have to look at a short sale because there are so many of them."

The contract in a short sale is normally contingent on the acceptance by the lender of the net proceeds from the sale as full payment for the debt on the property. This is the crucial element to such an arrangement because if the lender and the seller don't agree to this, then the sale cannot take place. Sometimes potential buyers find that the offer they make is acceptable to the seller but not to the seller's lender. The process of buying a short sale is essentially a three-way negotiation between the seller, the buyer, and the lender, instead of a typical two-way buyer-and-seller negotiation.

Under normal circumstances, when a home is sold the proceeds go to pay off the first mortgage (and a second mortgage or home equity loan if one exists), property taxes, a transfer tax, closing costs, and a commission to the listing agent. After these obligations have been paid, the sellers can keep any profit. In a short sale, the lender must agree to accept less than the total of all these obligations. Lenders will do this in order to avoid foreclosing on the home, which is also costly for banks in terms of lost revenue and the necessity of eventually selling the home.

Short Sale Buying Tips

- Be patient and flexible, particularly with the settlement date. Make sure you can continue to rent your home and have the ability to end the lease with thirty days notice in case the settlement date must be moved or the contract does not go to completion.

- Work with a Realtor experienced with short sales and an attorney who can make sure that all the paperwork, especially the title transfer and the release of any liens on the property are handled appropriately. The last thing a first-time buyer needs is to deal with the unpaid debts of the previous owner.

- Make sure to get an inspection. Homeowners who have been struggling to pay their bills are likely to have deferred important maintenance on their home. While adding a fresh coat of paint is a minor job for first-time homeowners, repairing the roof or replacing the furnace are expensive propositions that may be a budget-breaker for the household. A home inspector can evaluate the systems and appliances and provide an estimate of when things might need to be replaced.

- Pay careful attention to the details of the contract. When the sellers are in financial distress, there is a greater likelihood of items being removed from the home or damage occurring during their move.

Foreclosures

While purchasing a foreclosure can be more straightforward than buying a short sale, foreclosures are not always a breeze, either.

Tolbert says, "Foreclosures can be quicker than buying a short sale, you'll know in a few days if your offer is accepted. But many foreclosures are in terrible shape, with appliances missing, broken air-conditioning systems, and even vandalism. This means the financing will be harder to obtain, and the buyers may need more cash upfront to fix the place."

While buyers assume a foreclosure is being sold at a rock-bottom price, this is not always the case. The seller (in this case, the financial institution) wants to recoup as much of its investment as possible while still selling quickly. Sometimes banks will opt for an extremely low sales price to create a bidding war among potential buyers, which will drive up the price. Foreclosure buyers should ask their real estate agent to find out if there are other offers on the property so they can decide how much they're willing to offer in order to buy the home. The price depends on the local market and how aggressive the bank wants to be in selling the home.

David Kerr, a Realtor with ZipRealty, in the San Francisco area, says, "A lot of foreclosures can't be financed with FHA loans because the property must be in livable condition in order to qualify for this loan program."

Buyers should be prepared to find alternative financing to an FHA loan if they are looking at foreclosures or be patient and search for a home that's in good condition. Some loans are also available that wrap remodeling and repair costs into the price of the loan. Potential foreclosure buyers should ask their lender about the availability and requirements of such loan programs.

Foreclosures are typically sold "as is," since the seller is no longer a homeowner but a financial institution. Inspections are allowed and should be considered critical so the buyer can understand both the true condition of the property and the cost estimates of making the property livable. Not all foreclosures require extensive work, of course. Some are in perfect, move-in condition. Others will lack appliances, kitchen cabinets, light fixtures, and even flooring and may have damaged walls and missing heating and air-conditioning systems.

An experienced Realtor can help buyers evaluate whether a property is priced low enough to make the purchase and subsequent work required a good deal. Besides relying on your agent's expertise, buyers need to carefully consider whether they have the time and energy to either do some of the work themselves or to hire contractors who need to be supervised.

Hiring a licensed appraiser should also be considered. While the lender will have discounted the price of the property in order to sell it quickly, a licensed appraiser, who normally charges a few hundred dollars, can give the best unbiased estimate of a property's current market value. If the appraisal is significantly higher than the asking price for the house and the home is in good condition or you are willing and able to spend the time and money to make the necessary repairs to the property, purchasing a foreclosure can make sense. And, as Tolbert pointed out about short sales, in some parts of the country buyers have little else to buy besides foreclosures.

Foreclosure Buying Tips

- Be prepared by working with an agent experienced with foreclosure transactions. The agent should help you evaluate the foreclosure to determine whether the price is fair and whether this could be a good investment.

- Don't be surprised, especially in some parts of the country, to be bidding against other buyers for a foreclosure.

- Make sure you can arrange financing for a foreclosure. Properties in disrepair may be harder to finance.

- Have an inspection. Typically, foreclosures are sold "as is," meaning the buyer will be responsible for all home improvements and repairs, no matter how large or small.

- Hire an appraiser to evaluate the current market value of the home. This can give you a better sense of whether the asking price is a bargain or not.

Auctions

In addition to the standard way of purchasing a foreclosure, many lenders and even some individual sellers who want to sell their home quickly are opting to sell their property at an auction. There are both government and private auctions for properties, and some new home builders are opting to sell multiple properties at once through an auction. Auctions are especially popular with condominium developments when a builder wants to close-out the project and sell the remaining homes in one fell swoop rather than one at a time in a slow market.

Attending an auction can be wildly intimidating for a first-time home buyer, but working with a Realtor who knows the value of homes in a given neighborhood can help prepare the buyer for purchasing a home this way. Buyers are normally allowed to bring an agent with them to the auction, although it's not required. The advantage to buyers of purchasing a home at an auction is that the process is quick and doesn't require extended negotiations. Buyers bid on the property and the price of the winning bid is the price of the property. However, buyers need to be completely confident of their financial ability to purchase a home and their emotional ability to choose the right property and not get carried away by the excitement of a live auction. In most cases the deposit made by the winning bidder at any auction is nonrefundable.

Buyers well-versed in the type of house they want to buy and the location may want to consider purchasing a home at an auction in the hope of getting a bargain. However, auctions involve competitive bidding, and buyers need to be very aware of their budgetary limits. Buying a "bargain," say, a home priced originally at $600,000 for $450,000, may sound great. However, if you meant to limit yourself to homes priced under $400,000, you may have just dug yourself a financial hole that will be hard to get out of.

To start, buyers need to do their research. When an auction is advertised locally or found online, potential buyers need to determine the terms and conditions of the auction. Government-sponsored property auctions can be found at Treas.gov/auctions/treasury/rp. For private auctions, it's best to search online for "property auctions" in the county or city where you want to buy a home.

Detailed information can be found online about each auction and will tell you how to become an eligible bidder (usually you need to register ahead of time) and will explain financing requirements, including bid deposits, closing deadlines, and purchase-agreement provisions. Specific information about each property, including deposit requirements, is also available on the auction website.

Buyers should always view the property on which they wish to bid ahead of time either at a scheduled open house or by making an appointment with the listing broker. Your buyer's agent can also help you with this process. Find out if you can have a home inspection on the property; rules vary from auction company to auction company.

Auctions are normally identified as "absolute" or "reserve" auctions. An absolute auction means that the sellers agree to sell the home to the highest bidder regardless of the price. A reserve auction means that the property is being sold subject to seller approval.

Normally, in addition to the earnest money deposit of about 5% of the purchase price, buyers at an auction will be required to pay a "buyers premium," a percentage added to the bid amount (usually also about 5%) as the total contract price. Settlements usually take place within thirty to forty-five days after the seller's acceptance of the contract. If the buyers cannot secure financing by the closing date, they will lose their deposit.

Auction Buying Tips

- Before considering buying a home at an auction, be certain what type of home you want to buy: the features, the neighborhood, the price. Auctions move very fast, so buyers need to be thoroughly prepared and committed to the purchase.

- Get prequalified for financing before registering for an auction so you know your price range. If you have the winning bid, you will need to be ready with approved financing within thirty to forty-five days of the auction for the settlement.

- Realize that most deposits at auctions are nonrefundable for any reason, even if you cannot obtain financing.

- Preview the property or properties on which you intend to bid before the auction either at an open house or by appointment. Consult with a Realtor to determine what the fair-market value of the home should be so you can compare this with the bidding prices. Many auction websites will provide detailed information about the property being placed on auction, so review all these materials carefully to be sure you know what you're buying. For instance, if you're buying a condominium or a home within a homeowner's association, be sure you can afford the monthly fees in addition to your other homeownership expenses.

- Find out if you can have a home inspection on the property and arrange for one prior to the auction if you can.

- Review all the information available on the auction website about the auction process, including registration, materials needed the day of the auction, and what fees to expect to pay.

- Be very firm with your budgetary limits: don't get carried away by the excitement of the bidding and end up with a home you cannot afford.

✓ CHECKLIST

- ❑ If you're considering making an offer on a short sale, be prepared for the process to be slow and frustrating, with the potential for the offer to be rejected after months of waiting.

- ❑ Be aware that foreclosures are sold "as is." Even if the property looks like a bargain, have a home inspection and estimate the additional costs of repairs.

- ❑ Make sure you can obtain financing for a short sale or foreclosure; this can be more difficult if the property is in bad condition.

- ❑ Be wary of purchasing a home at auction: do lots of research on the auction process and the property on which you want to bid. Be sure to stick firmly to a budget before buying. Understand that a deposit made at an auction is normally nonrefundable.

CHAPTER EIGHT

Contracts and Contingencies: Get Everything in Writing

As Debbie watched the prices tumbling on the condominiums in the neighborhood she loved, she realized that she should make an attempt to buy one. She felt secure in her job, had been saving faithfully for years, and had built up a substantial stash of cash and investments. Debbie hired a Realtor and got prequalified for a loan. Since she already knew which building she hoped to live in, Debbie was ready to make an offer within a week or so of deciding to take the plunge into homeownership.

Debbie fell in love with a two-bedroom, two-bath home on the tenth floor with a view of the city's rooftops, but the asking price was $500,000. She intended to spend no more than $425,000. Debbie's Realtor counseled her against it, but Debbie insisted on offering $400,000 for the condo, assuming that she had the upper hand in this buyer's market. The seller rejected the offer instantly and refused to negotiate at all with Debbie or her agent. Convinced that this was just an obstinate seller, Debbie made two more lowball offers on other condominiums in the development, which were also rejected. Eventually, Debbie's agent convinced her that she had to make a reasonable offer in order to begin negotiations. Debbie was able to purchase a smaller place on a lower floor after making an opening *offer that was just 5% below the asking price. While she had to compromise on the size of her home, she was satisfied to be living in the building she wanted and staying within her budget.*

Making an Offer

In a buyer's market, first-time buyers in particular sometimes assume that because they have the upper hand in negotiations, they can make any offer at all and it will be accepted. Buyers in this risky economic environment think that because they are taking the risk of buying a property that may or may not go up in value, sellers should just be grateful for an offer at all.

But buyers need to recognize that how their offer is viewed depends on the sellers' motivations for putting their home on the market. Some homeowners need to sell in order to move out of their area for a job or to downsize into a less-expensive home if their income has dropped. In those instances, sellers will be highly motivated to sell and may be willing to accept a low offer. But homeowners putting their homes on the market because they are nearing retirement and want to downsize or because they want to take advantage of lower prices and buy something larger are much more likely to hold out for a full-price offer.

Diane Williams, an associate broker with Weichert Realtors, in Springhouse, Pennsylvania, says that buyers need to have their Realtor look up all the comparable sales, called "comps" by many real estate agents, of similar homes nearby in order to evaluate what the first offer should be.

"The Realtor should also look to see how long the home has been on the market, which makes a huge difference in how willing the sellers are to negotiate," says Williams. "Also you need to know if there have been any price changes. I always ask the listing agent about the sellers to see what their hot buttons are. For instance, it's a good idea to see if the settlement date is crucial to them, because if it is, the buyers may be able to offer less money if they can go to closing on the right date."

Williams says that buyers should be wary of making a lowball offer, since some sellers may be insulted by the offer and refuse to negotiate .

"Deciding whether to make a lowball offer depends on how much the buyers like the property," says Williams. "If they really want it, then they should make a realistic offer based on the comps. "

David Kerr, a Realtor with ZipRealty, in the San Francisco area, says that the key to moving from a "wanna-be" buyer to a homeowner is to pull together competing interests.

"What you can afford and what you are comfortable spending are two totally separate things, just like what the seller wants you to pay and what the buyer wants to spend," says Kerr. "You need to find a meeting place for all these interests."

Kerr says that making a lowball offer risks an outright rejection from the seller.

"This doesn't matter if you don't care that deeply about the house, but if this is the home you want to buy, you could lose it," says Kerr. "With an REO or foreclosure, a bank will likely reject a lowball offer outright, since they have usually listed the home at a low price."

Kerr says that in order to determine a reasonable offer, buyers need to ask their agent to research all the statistics on recent sales in the neighborhood. It's particularly important to look at how many of them came in above or below or close to the asking price.

Some buyers want to automatically offer 10% under the asking price or use some other formula, but a strategic offer is more complicated than that.

"It is an old-fashioned way of thinking to offer a certain percentage below the asking price," says Kerr. "You really need to look at the numbers, so that's why it's so important to know the market."

Realtor Jessie L. Brown with Weichert Realtors, in Charlotte, North Carolina, says that he and his colleagues typically do a twelve-month analysis of a home a client wants to make an offer on as well as similar homes.

"It's important to do a thorough market analysis so that the buyer really knows the value of the property," says Brown. "You need to know if the home has already been reduced in price several times or if homes are selling at close to the asking price in that particular neighborhood."

Brown says that making an offer on a HUD-owned foreclosure offers a different scenario than making an offer on a home occupied by the homeowner. He says a lowball offer on a government-owned (as opposed to a bank-owned) foreclosure is expected.

"Buyers need to realize they are not buying a deal, they are buying a home," says Brown. "If a buyer has an emotional attachment to a house, you don't want them to make a lowball offer that the seller rejects as unrealistic."

However, Brown also works hard to get his clients into a home at a reasonable price so that they will be building equity in the home right from the start.

"I want my clients to walk into a home with equity of 10 to 15%. So even if they only have an FHA loan with a down payment of 3.5%, I try to get them to buy a home for less than the appraised value," says Brown.

Earnest Money Deposits

In addition to deciding on the appropriate offer, buyers need to present an "earnest money deposit" with their signed contract. The earnest money deposit will be held in an escrow account until the settlement date, so the sellers and agents will be unable to touch it until all the final documents are signed that transfer ownership from one person to the next. This deposit becomes part of the down payment, the rest of which will be made at the settlement.

How much should you give as an earnest money deposit? This depends a lot on whether there is competition for the home you want to buy. If there is more than one offer for the house or you simply want to be absolutely certain that your offer is accepted because you have fallen in love with the house, the earnest money deposit should be as large as possible. The point of this deposit is to demonstrate to the sellers that you are a serious buyer with the financial ability to purchase their home.

In most cases, this deposit ranges from 1 to 5% of the price of the house. This will also vary depending on how large a down payment you intend to make. For buyers using an FHA loan, which requires a 3.5% down payment, an earnest money deposit of 1 or 2% should be fine. But if you're buying a home with 20% down, it makes more sense to make the earnest money deposit 5 or even 10%.

Make sure you understand that you can lose your deposit if you do not fulfill your obligations under the contract. Your agent should work with you to make sure this doesn't happen.

Contingencies

Buyers often assume that price is the only negotiating point in a contract, and while it's usually the key element, it's not the only one.

Antoinette Matisoo, a broker Realtor from Holden, Massachusetts, says that no contract can go forward at all without a prequalification letter for the buyer from a reputable lender. Negotiating cannot begin until the financing has been approved.

"Next, buyers need to be ready to talk about how quickly a closing can occur. They need to know when they will be ready to move, how much notice they need to give their landlord, and when the loan will be ready to close before they can negotiate a closing date with a seller," says Matisoo.

During the height of the housing boom and homebuying frenzy in 2004 and 2005, many buyers were offering "noncontingent" contracts, meaning that if the seller accepted the offer there would be no other factors that could stop the contract from going to completion. Today, contracts typically are contingent on the buyer obtaining financing, the completion of a satisfactory home inspection, and the completion of a home appraisal, which values the home at or above the sales price. In some jurisdictions, a satisfactory termite inspection and a satisfactory radon test must also be completed before settlement. In this case, either the tests must be negative or the sellers must treat the problem. Buyers who currently own a home often also include a contingency requiring the sale of their existing home prior to settlement.

Appraisals

One of the most important contingencies in this current market is the appraisal contingency, which allows buyers to be released from the contract and have their deposit returned if the appraisal is not high enough. With home values adjusting rapidly in some markets and most homes around the country having reduced values, appraisals are sometimes coming in for less than the contract price.

A similar problem occurred at the height of the recent housing boom, when frenzied buyers competing for homes were often escalating their offers above the property value. In those days, when buyers rarely signed a contract with any contingency at all, the buyers simply had to find a way to make up the difference between the appraised value (which is the maximum loan for that property allowed by the lender) and their offer. In other words, if the home was appraised at $550,000 and the buyer had offered $600,000, the buyer had to come up with an additional $50,000 to buy the home.

Today's market conditions, which favor buyers, are easier on the buyer's finances.

Kerr says, "As long as the appraisal contingency is intact, then the buyers can cancel the contract if the appraisal comes in too low, or they can renegotiate to a lower price. In this current market, sellers are actually willing to do that. Another option, which isn't always possible, is to have a second appraisal done."

Appraisers are typically hired by the lender rather than the buyer or the buyer's agent, so the buyer and the seller have little or no control over the appraisal.

"Sometimes agents need to ask about the reasons for a low appraisal and make sure that this is not automatically being done because the home is in a declining market," says Kerr. "For instance, if the appraiser is not local, he or she may not know that a big difference in home values occurs because of being above or below a particular street or within a certain school district. Sometimes the agent or the lender just needs to be pushy. But if the appraiser has come through the bank and is an in-house appraiser, then there's not much the buyer can do."

Angie Hicks, founder of Angie's List, says that buyers should always make certain they are protected with an appraisal contingency in any purchase contract.

"That way, if the appraisal comes in lower than the asking price, the buyer can work with the seller on reducing the asking price so it falls in line with the appraisal value, or take his/her earnest money and walk away from the deal," says Hicks. "If the buyer did not include an appraisal contingency in the contract and the appraisal comes in lower than the asking price, the buyer is responsible to come up with the monetary difference to make the financing work."

Jim Savitz, a real estate attorney with Village Settlements in Gaithersburg, Maryland, says that some FHA loans require two appraisals, both paid for by the buyer, in order to make sure a property has the value to justify the loan.

Savitz says, "If an appraisal comes in too low, there are two basic options. One is for the buyer to come up with the extra cash to cover the gap between the approved amount of the loan and the contract price. But, much more likely in the current market—if the seller is rational—is that the seller has the option to reduce the price to the appraised value."

Barbara Reynolds, president of marketing for Howard Hanna Realty Services, in Cleveland, Ohio, says, "Banks are more conservative than they were in the past, particularly in neighborhoods with decreasing values. If an appraisal comes in low, buyers and sellers can ask for a re-appraisal. The Realtor should provide comparable sales statistics to substantiate the price of the house. If the second appraisal is still too low, the sellers will have to adjust the price to accommodate the appraisal."

Home Inspections

Many states require home sellers to complete a "disclaimer" or a "disclosure" form, which reveals their knowledge of the condition of the home. While buyers should review these forms to see what sellers can share about the systems, appliances, and functionality of the residence, these forms should never be a substitute for a homebuyer paying for a professional home inspection. Homebuyers should insist on a contract contingent on a satisfactory home inspection. Before the housing bubble burst, when buyers were competing with each other for homes, most opted not to have a home inspection. Or, if they did, it was an "information-only" inspection, which meant that they could gather facts about the condition of the home after they had made an offer. Even if they found major flaws in the property, they were required to fulfill the terms of the contract once it was accepted.

Now that the playing field is level, or even sloped in the direction of buyers, home inspections are almost always part of the contract. A home inspection is vital for two reasons: first, it allows the buyers the option of discovering appliances or systems in need of repair, so they can ask the sellers to make the repairs, reduce their offer on the basis of the cost of the repairs, or even withdraw the offer. Second, buyers can use the home inspection as a time to learn how to maintain their potential new home and get an idea of when certain appliances or systems might need replacement. Many home inspectors will make suggestions for minor improvements (or even major ones), which can increase the functionality and value of the home, such as recaulking a tub or adding a tile backsplash behind the stove. Homebuyers should attend the home inspection with a notebook and pen so they are ready to take notes on suggested home improvements, although the home inspector will also provide a report on his findings.

Savitz says, "All buyers should get a home inspection and if the property is bank-owned, the bank almost prefers that you get one so you are prepared. Banks recognize the wisdom of a purchaser understanding the condition of the property before deciding to go forward with a contract. This is more crucial than ever with foreclosures."

Hicks says that buyers would be wise to do some research on home inspectors even before they make an offer for a home.

"Once the contract has been signed, there will be a time limit for getting an inspection done, so buyers should find two or three home inspectors in case one is not available," says Hicks. "It may seem silly to go to the trouble of researching a good home inspector, since this is only a $200 or $300 purchase, but that purchase is helping you decide on one of the most significant investments of your life."

Hicks says that not all states license home inspectors, but she recommends that buyers should check for a license if they do. Hicks recommends searching for an inspector who is a member of either the National Association of Home Inspectors (NAHI.org) or the American Society of Home Inspectors (ASHI.org), both of which require demonstrated experience as an inspector.

Other tips on home inspections from Angie's List (AngiesList.com):

- Make sure the home inspector has errors and omissions insurance, which can protect the company and you if you have a claim.

- Find out when you will receive the finished report, and ask to see a sample home inspection report to get an idea of what's included and how issues are described or rated by the inspector.

- Find out what is included in the inspection and be prepared to pay extra for a termite inspection and radon inspection. Not all inspections include the roof, so be sure to check if this will be part of the inspection.

- Attend the inspection so you know what they have looked at and to get to know the house. A good inspector will share with you how long to expect some appliances and systems to last, and provide maintenance tips.

Brian Fricke, a certified financial planner with Financial Management Concepts, in Winter Springs, Florida, and author of *Worry Free Retirement*, says that first-time homebuyers don't realize how much they need to budget for repairs and maintenance. He recommends asking the home inspector for an idea of how long the roof will last and how much it will cost to replace it, along with appliances and other systems. Some home inspectors can even offer energy-saving tips and estimate the cost of installing items such as a programmable thermostat or replacing the windows with a more energy-efficient product.

Using the Realtor's Home Inspector

While some buyers prefer to find their own home inspectors by asking friends and colleagues for recommendations, it's far more common for buyers to work with the professionals suggested by their Realtors such as home inspectors and settlement companies and even lenders.

"There's a consumer-friendly law which requires disclosure in writing if the real estate brokerage has a relationship with a recommended business, such as a settlement company or mortgage lender," says Trudy Severa, a Realtor with Long & Foster Real Estate, in Reston, Virginia. "Many consumers like the idea of 'one-stop shopping,' with everything handled by one company. But it needs to be made very clear that there is no requirement to use a recommended business."

The Real Estate Settlement Procedures Act (RESPA) requires that real estate brokers disclose an ownership interest or affiliation with a mortgage lender, a settlement company, or any other real estate-related business. Real estate agents do not receive any financial benefit when you choose to work with an affiliated business.

Rich Davila, a Realtor and Washington, D.C., district director for ZipRealty says that working with recommended lenders and others can make a transaction smoother.

"The key is that we do not accept anything from these affiliated businesses, not even dinner," says Davila. "All I get is a decision-makers' cell phone number, and that's all I want. By law, we must make multiple recommendations. Consumers need to ask agents whether they are getting anything from these recommended businesses, such as a rebate or some kind of commission. If they are, the consumers should drop that agent."

Home-Warranty Programs

While not often a make-or-break issue with a contract, buyers, especially those who have not owned a home before, often request a home warranty. Many sellers automatically include a home warranty in the contract because they are reassuring to buyers, and they also cover the seller while their home is on the market.

Unfortunately, home-warranty programs are not always what buyers hope.

Hicks says, "A lot of home sellers now pay for warranty programs, but these are some of the most complained-about programs on Angie's List. Mostly this is because people are unclear about what is covered and what's not. Some people get confused and think that because they have had a home inspection, they are automatically covered under a home-warranty program. These are two completely separate things."

Hicks says buyers need to read the warranty coverage and understand what is covered. She says that warranty programs are worth having as long as the consumers know how the program works, especially if the warranty is paid for by the seller.

Matisoo says, "Buyers are really more concerned with money than with a home warranty. You have to know what's covered under the warranty to determine whether it's worth much to have it."

Reynolds has a more positive opinion about home-warranty programs, suggesting that buyers ask for the sellers to buy one if they haven't offered it. She says that buyers should even consider paying for one themselves if the sellers won't.

Home-warranty programs range in price according to the area where the home is located and what is covered, but they average $300 to $400 for a single-family home in most parts of the country for one year's coverage. Most programs also have a deductible, which varies, usually starting at $100.

Savitz says home warranties can offer peace of mind for homebuyers, so they can be valuable for that factor alone.

"Home warranties are okay, but you're required to go through the home-warranty company and use their contractors, which can cause delay and not allow the homeowner to have control over the situation," says Savitz.

Hicks says that the control issue is the main reason consumers complain about a home-warranty program.

"The warranty company controls who they send and whether they repair or replace something," says Hicks. "For instance, warranty programs usually only last one or two years, so the company may decide to repair a refrigerator to keep it working until the warranty ends. But it may be smarter for the consumer to skip paying the deductible and just buy a new appliance."

What Conveys?

In addition to paying attention to what appliances and systems may be covered under a home-warranty program, buyers need to list in the contract those items that they expect to convey with the property at settlement. Few moments are worse for a brand-new homeowner than arriving at the walk-through home inspection just before the settlement only to discover that the washer and dryer are missing, along with all the window blinds and the dining room chandelier.

While the assumption made by most buyers is that appliances that have been installed and custom-installed window treatments automatically come with the house, this is not the case. Experienced agents will remind their buyers that they need to ask, in writing, in the initial purchase contract, for the inclusion of all items they want to stay. Light fixtures are one of the most common items to be changed out as one set of owners leaves and another moves in; so if the buyers particularly like a chandelier or wall sconce, they need to put the request for the item to convey with the house in writing.

Sellers may not always agree to convey everything the buyers asks for, especially if the chandelier in question has sentimental value. This should be part of the negotiating process. Additionally, if buyers want certain items removed from the property, this should be put in writing. For example, if the backyard has a shabby swing set, the sellers may want to just leave this behind. But if the buyers don't want the set and don't want to deal with the hassle and expense of removing such an awkward item, they can request in writing that the swing set be removed.

One of the glitches that can derail a settlement is when items that are written into the contract as conveying with the house are missing. But at least in this case, the buyers and the buyers' agent can point to the signed contract and negotiate for the missing items to be returned or for financial compensation to replace the items.

Keep in mind, though, that foreclosures are sold "as is," so that buyers will not be compensated for any missing items, even ones that normally convey with a home such as the kitchen cabinets.

Home inspections, appraisals, home-warranty programs and written contracts all offer protection for homebuyers, protections that are needed more than ever during an economic crisis. Buyers and their agents just need to make sure they follow all the steps correctly to ensure that these protections are in place.

✓ CHECKLIST

❑ Before making a lowball offer, consider carefully how much you want to purchase this particular property. The danger of a lowball offer is that the seller will be insulted and reject it, and then refuse to negotiate at all.

❑ Work with your Realtor to evaluate comparable sales in order to come up with a reasonable offer. Look at how long the home has been on the market, recent sales prices of similar homes, and how closely the sales prices correlate with the asking prices.

❑ Have your Realtor talk with the listing agent for your potential new home to ask whether the sellers want a particular settlement date or have other considerations that you could use to make your offer more acceptable.

❑ Make sure your contract is contingent on an appraisal that values the home at your offer or higher.

❑ Make your offer contingent on a satisfactory home inspection.

❑ Attend the home inspection and ask the home inspector to give you an estimate of when appliances or systems may need replacing, along with an estimate of the cost. Take notes at the home inspection and ask for maintenance tips.

❑ Ask the seller to pay for a home-warranty program for at least one year. Read the warranty-program paperwork to make sure you understand what is covered.

❑ Put everything in writing that you want to convey with the home, and make sure the sellers have agreed to convey the listed items.

CHAPTER NINE

Insurance Issues

When Marcy bought her first home in Charlotte, North Carolina, she thought she had everything covered: she obtained a loan and bought a foreclosure with a 20% down payment. Marcy moved in and began improving the home with new appliances, hardwood flooring, and fresh paint. A few months later, she received a legal document that questioned her right to own the property. Apparently, the foreclosure had taken place without the knowledge of the owner's wife, whose name had been on the title of the property but not on the mortgage. A clerk had not noticed the second name on the title, and the homeowner neglected to mention her existence since the couple had been separated for years.

Once the couple began divorce proceedings, the wife became aware of the loss of the house and insisted she still had a claim on the property because her name was on the title. At her closing, Marcy's settlement company had mentioned the existence of owner's title insurance, but she opted not to buy it in order to save some extra money to spend on her new home. Now that the title was in dispute, Marcy's lender was protected by the standard title insurance, but Marcy had to pay substantial lawyer's fees to make sure she was able to protect her right to own the home. If she had to give up title to the home, she would lose

*the equity of her 20% down payment and the additional money she
had spent on the property, which came to over $10,000.*

First-time homebuyers may think they can sit back and relax
once they have a signed contract and the owners have accepted
their offer, especially once they've had a home inspection and
are satisfied with the condition of the property. But the time
between the ratified (accepted) contract and the settlement
date requires vigilance and activity on the part of the buyers.

First-time homebuyers often find confusing the variety of
insurance coverage required in order to become a homeowner.
It's important to understand the differences between these
insurance policies and not only what they cover, but *who* they
cover. In many cases, while the homebuyers must pay for the
coverage, it's actually the financial institution lending the
money (bank, credit union, or mortgage company) that's
protected by the insurance.

Types of Insurance

- Private Mortgage Insurance (PMI)
- Mortgage Insurance Premium (MIP)
- Home-Warranty Program
- Homeowners or Hazard Insurance
- Flood Insurance
- Optional Homeowners Insurance Coverage
- Title Insurance
- Owner's Title Insurance

Private Mortgage Insurance (PMI)

Protects the lender against the borrower defaulting on the loan. This
insurance is generally charged by the lender on conventional

loans when the buyers have made a down payment of 20% or less. The insurance premium is normally paid on a monthly basis as part of the mortgage payment, but buyers may want to arrange with their lenders to make a lump-sum upfront mortgage insurance payment at the settlement or to arrange to wrap it into the loan so that it becomes a tax-deductible expense. With some income limitations, even monthly PMI premiums are now tax-deductible. (See Chapter Two on financing for more details.)

Mortgage Insurance Premium (MIP)

Protects the lender against the borrower defaulting on the loan. This is a one-time, upfront mortgage insurance payment required by FHA loans, in addition to monthly PMI payments.

Home-Warranty Program

Protects the homeowners. This insurance does not protect the home itself, but provides insurance to repair or replace the appliances and systems in the home. A home-warranty program is not required by the lender but is an optional protection provided by the home sellers or the homebuyers. Home-warranty programs usually last for one or two years. Some may be renewable by the homeowners.

Homeowners or Hazard Insurance

Protects the homeowners' assets and also protects the lender because this means the asset on which the loan has been based (the home) is replaceable. Obtaining homeowners insurance (also known as hazard insurance in many areas) is the most important step after the home inspection. Most mortgage lenders will not approve a loan without the proof of homeowners insurance, which must be presented at the settlement. This insurance, normally paid as part of the monthly mortgage payment, provides protection against fire or water damage and natural disasters, which could damage or destroy a home, such as a tree falling on the roof during a tropical storm or a portion of the roof being torn off during a tornado. Insurance claims don't have to be tied to a major disaster, either, but can help homeowners make repairs in other situations such as a plumbing leak that causes drywall and flooring damage.

Angie Hicks, founder of Angie's List, a consumer group that provides members with information about local contractors and companies, says that homebuyers should talk to an insurance agent who can estimate the appropriate coverage for the property and the residents' belongings. She recommends comparing policies and rates from multiple companies or working with an independent insurance agent who can do this for consumers. Many consumers start by checking with the insurance company that provides their auto insurance since most companies offer discounts for customers with multiple policies.

"For homeowners insurance, you need to be sure you're getting replacement coverage, not current value, since replacement costs can be considerably higher," says Hicks. "Because homeowners insurance is rolled into your mortgage payment, people often forget about it. But it should be reviewed annually to make sure your coverage is appropriate just like any other insurance you have."

Hicks recommends checking with AccuCoverage.com to determine whether the homeowners insurance is at the appropriate level. The Insurance Information Institute (III.org) quotes a 2006 Insurance Research Council poll, which found that 96% of homeowners had homeowners insurance, while 43% of renters had renters insurance. Since homeowners are required to purchase insurance coverage by their mortgage companies, they often accept the basic policy without reviewing their options. The basic coverage insures the home and the homeowners' belongings up to a certain level.

"Insurance companies are not concerned about your home's land value; they want to make sure they have enough coverage to rebuild the home," says Jonathan Porwick, an insurance agent with State Farm, in Chevy Chase, Maryland. "For example, a home worth $500,000 may only be insured for $300,000. In this case, the land value would be $200,000."

Porwick says that insurance companies have tools to determine the level of coverage needed, and homeowners themselves can also review the appraisal of their home, which separates the value of the land from the rebuilding cost. On many appraisals, there is a section called "cost to rebuild new."

"It's not an exact science to determine the required level of homeowners insurance," says Porwick. "Homeowners should utilize both appraisals and insurance company tools. However, homeowners should go with what they are comfortable with in terms of coverage. The key is to make sure the policy will replace the home."

Porwick says that State Farm currently adds a 20% cushion on top of the amount of coverage on the home. This would be utilized in case construction costs have risen or some other problem causes the replacement price of the home to rise. For a $300,000 insurance policy, the home is actually insured up to $360,000.

"An important distinction in coverage is whether companies use 'similar construction' or 'common construction,'" says Porwick. "That's something you find in the fine print of the policy. As far as I would guess, 99% of insurance companies do 'similar construction,' but it is still wise to check on this."

"Similar construction" means that the home will be repaired or rebuilt back to the way it was, or at least as close to the actual construction as possible. A "common construction" policy means any materials deemed appropriate by the insurance company could be used to rebuild a home.

"In an area where there are many older homes, it is particularly important to have a similar construction policy. Many older homes have plaster walls. A policy with similar construction coverage would give the homeowner the option to rebuild using plaster again," says Porwick.

Flood Insurance

Protects the homeowners' assets and also protects the lender because this means the asset on which the loan has been based (the home) is replaceable. This insurance is required only for homes located within a flood zone as identified by the federal government. If the property is located within a flood zone, the lender will require flood insurance in addition to the protection of homeowners insurance. If at a later date, the federal government ever decides that the area surrounding your home is a flood zone, the lender will require flood insurance at that time.

Optional Homeowners Insurance Coverage

While the lender will require basic homeowners insurance, the buyer should also consider expanding their coverage to make sure they are fully protected in the event of an accident or emergency.

Personal property is covered by homeowners insurance up to a limit specified in the policy. Porwick says State Farm coverage is at least 75% of the insured value of the home. For example, for a home valued at $300,000 for insurance purposes, the personal property would be insured up to $225,000.

"I encourage everyone to do a complete home inventory and take pictures of everything in their home to make sure their personal property is covered," says Porwick. "This is especially important if you buy expensive items such as high-tech equipment, art, or jewelry. The level of personal property coverage can be increased easily for a minimal amount of increased premium."

For example, Porwick says that jewelry is typically covered up to $2,500 per piece and to $5,000 aggregate. Jewelry valued higher than $2,500 should be insured with a separate rider to the policy. Similarly, artwork, furs, and expensive high-tech equipment may also need to be separately insured.

Beyond protecting the value of personal items and the standard insurance coverage for the house itself, homebuyers should research ways to customize their policy to cover potential problems.

While flood insurance is only required by lenders for properties located within a flood zone identified by the federal government, Porwick says that some homeowners are choosing to purchase flood insurance even if they are not living in a flood zone. Flood insurance can be obtained through FEMA's (Federal Emergency Management Agency) National Flood Insurance Program.

Hicks recommends that consumers make sure they have a "loss of use" rider, similar to rental car coverage on auto insurance, which would pay for a short-term rental or hotel stay if the home is uninhabitable while being repaired.

Porwick says that homeowners should check the level of their loss-of-use coverage to be sure it's adequate. This coverage will pay for you to live in another dwelling while your home is being repaired. Some companies put a time or monetary cap on this coverage. A large family may want to make sure they have enough coverage to pay for several bedrooms in a motel or long-term-stay suite, rather than enough for just one standard motel room.

Porwick also recommends that consumers review their policy to be sure it includes inflation coverage, which automatically increases the limits of their insurance coverage to reflect rising costs of construction and repair work.

Another important optional coverage is back-up sewer and drain protection, which provides coverage for the clean-up required if a pipe in the home backs up, the water company has a back-up on the street, or even if a sump pump gives out.

When purchasing homeowners insurance, consumers have the option of choosing the amount of their deductible. The lower the deductible, the higher the cost of insurance.

"When I first started in the insurance business, more people took the lower deductible, but now, in part because of the high cost of housing, more people are opting for a $1,000 deductible," says Porwick.

Porwick says that sensitivity to the issue of putting in too many claims also enters into the deductible decision. Some homeowners have lost their insurance coverage or experienced a dramatic increase in their insurance costs because they consistently requested reimbursement from their insurance company for minor repairs or made dubious claims.

"At a $1,000 deductible, people are embracing the concept of self-insuring a little more, and they can save a lot of money on their policy," says Porwick.

Condominium buyers may assume that their condominium fees include insurance coverage, but they still need to purchase coverage for the inside of their home and for their personal property. Condominium owners pay for insurance on their building through their condominium association fee, but they need to carry additional insurance to cover any exclusions on the community policy. For example, if a water main break causes damage to the exterior of the condominium building or to the parking garage, the necessary repairs would be covered by the association's insurance. But if a dishwasher broke down and overflowed within someone's condominium unit, the homeowner would be responsible for paying for the repairs.

Title Insurance

Protects the lender up to the value of the loan on the property. This insurance is required by lenders to protect against a potential claim against your rightful ownership of the property. Title insurance means that the title company will defend your ownership and protect against financial loss caused by a title defect.

Owner's Title Insurance

Protects the owners in case of a title dispute. If the title to your property is disputed, the standard title insurance policy will protect the lender up to the value of the mortgage. But as you own a home longer and build up equity, the burden of a title dispute falls on you. Owner's title insurance can protect the owner's assets up to the value of the policy.

"Holding title" to a property simply means that the people named in the title have the right to possess, occupy, and sell that property subject to restrictions placed on the property by government or other legal authorities, such as a homeowners association. Title is typically transferred by a deed, which is recorded with the local government. When someone purchases a property, the settlement attorney or title company searches the land records of the county or city where the residence is located for "title defects." Title defects are anything in the history of the property that could impact the legal ownership of the property. If a title defect is discovered, it could cause the loss of some or all of the owner's land to the ownership claim of someone else.

While all this sounds like a lot of legalese, which should be left to lawyers, title problems can and do occur. Sometimes title disputes occur because of fraud or forgery, when someone illegally presents themselves as the owners of a property that doesn't belong to them. Other title disputes occur because of wills not being properly probated, missing or undisclosed heirs, or even owners not disclosing their marital status. Sometimes title disputes come up because of human error: the names on two documents are similar and so papers are mishandled, or the power of attorney has expired, or someone made a simple clerical mistake.

The worst type of title dispute involves the entire property, but sometimes these problems can crop up over a sliver of land that is claimed by two neighbors. When buyers purchase a townhome, a single-family home, or any style of a detached home (anything not in a condominium or co-op building), the lender will require a "house location survey," which shows the legal boundaries of the land being purchased. Buyers can also opt for a more detailed "boundary survey" by a licensed surveyor, which shows the location of improvements and structures within the borders of the property. Title disputes can sometimes occur because a survey has not been correctly done, and so one neighbor will have to buy out the other's strip of land or the land will revert to the neighboring owner automatically. This can become extremely complicated when the land in question includes a fence or a garage, which must be moved. Even worse was a case in Northern Virginia when a swimming pool had been built slightly over the property line. The neighbors insisted that the swimming pool be re-dug and moved over by a foot at considerable expense to the homeowners.

Ralph McMillan, a real estate attorney with McMillan-Terry, in Charlotte, North Carolina, says, "The most important thing in this market is that every homebuyer should purchase owners' title insurance. An owner's title insurance pays out 100% to the owner if there are any problems with the title. In this market, with short sales in particular, owner's title insurance is vital because title disputes are more common."

Jim Savitz, a real estate attorney with Village Settlements, in Gaithersburg, Maryland, says, "In the past, I always felt that buyers would be better off if they purchased their own title insurance coverage, not just the coverage that protects the lender. But now, everyone should buy it, particularly with bank-owned properties. It is crucial for homeowners to have this protection."

Buying a foreclosure, a short sale, or a home at an auction does sometimes complicate the title search.

Savitz says, "Foreclosures are often done by out-of-state companies who are not always aware of local issues that need to be taken care of, which then crop up at the settlement table. Sometimes, buried in the addendum on bank-owned properties will be a comment that means that the bank has a doubt about the insurability of the title. The buyer could end up with a title that is not as spotless as they might like."

Title insurance costs vary from state to state, according to Savitz.

"In Virginia, for example, it is a negotiable expense. In Maryland, there are two levels of policies. The higher level policy costs roughly $4.20 per $1,000 insured," says Savitz.

McMillan says, in North Carolina, owners title insurance runs about $2 per every $1,000 covered, so about $200 for a $100,000 house.

"It is well worth the cost for the peace of mind you have that you are covered if someone makes a claim on your title," says McMillan. "Each state has different requirements and regulations about insurance, but in every state you should make sure to get this coverage."

✓ CHECKLIST

❏ Make sure you understand the difference between mortgage insurance, homeowners insurance, home-warranty programs, and title insurance.

❏ As soon as the home inspection is done and the contract has been accepted, check with an insurance agent, your auto insurance company, and/or other insurance companies to compare rates for homeowners insurance.

❏ Do an inventory of your personal belongings, and discuss them with the insurance company you have chosen to make sure you are adequately covered.

❏ Purchase owner's title insurance in addition to the title insurance that covers the lender.

CHAPTER TEN

Legal and Tax Implications of Homebuying

When Barbara and Bob bought their first home, it was a stretch to make the monthly payments since they were about $400 per month more than their monthly rent had been. The mortgage broker who helped them qualify for a loan suggested that they change the level of federal income taxes being withheld from their paychecks in order to make their cash flow easier. Without consulting a tax advisor or an accountant, the couple made the assumption that since their mortgage broker said they would be getting a big refund on their taxes due to the deductions available to homeowners, they should make life simpler and just have $400 less taken out in taxes each month.

Now they were able to make their mortgage payments more easily, although they did worry a little that they had such a tiny sum of money in their savings account since they had made a down payment on their house and paid for closing costs and some new furniture. Assuming they would be getting a big tax refund, Barbara and Bob also ran up a credit card bill to make some home improvements. When April came, they were in for a rude awakening. Not only did they not have a generous refund check arriving, they actually owed money on their taxes.

They had blithely had too little taxes withheld for almost ten months, leaving them with an IRS bill of about $2,000. This bill wiped *out the couple's savings completely and then they had to readjust their withholding upward so they didn't have the same experience in the following tax year. Bob started working a second job on the weekends, and they put themselves on a strict budget in order to make ends meet. In the end, they were relieved that they were able to hold onto their home and pay off their tax bill, too.*

While this couple experienced a frustrating and confusing tax situation, almost all first-time homebuyers find the tax and legal implications of buying a home a bit overwhelming. In these trying times, when keeping a job and maintaining some financial security are so crucial, buyers may be tempted to save a little money by avoiding hiring an attorney, an accountant, a financial planner, or a tax advisor. But the old adage, "you've got to spend a little to save a lot" could hold true in the case of a first-time homebuyer, particularly if there are any unusual circumstances in the way the home is being purchased.

Tax Issues

Buying a home can be a boon to taxpayers because the federal government allows several deductions that are available only to homeowners. Most first-time homebuyers will find that buying a home will significantly reduce both their federal and state income tax liabilities. Homeowners can deduct their mortgage interest payments, points paid at settlement, and property taxes. Additional benefits may be available for first-time homebuyers, who can sometimes take advantage of state and local government tax credits geared to first-time buyers. (See appendix.)

For example, in Washington, D.C., a special tax credit is available for buyers who have purchased a home for the first-time in the city. This tax credit could be fully deductible or partially reduced depending on the income of the buyers.

In addition to the standard federal tax deductions available to all homeowners, the federal government added an $8,000 tax credit for first-time homebuyers in 2009. Although this tax credit applies only to homes purchased prior to December 1, 2009, additional federal tax credits for homebuyers could be part of future economic stimulus packages. Be sure to check the IRS website (IRS.gov) for updates on available tax credits and deductions for first-time homebuyers.

Most people think that first-time homebuyers are only those who have never owned a home, but this is not true. First-time buyers are defined by the federal government as those who have not owned a home in the previous three tax years.

Michael Martin, an enrolled agent certified by the IRS and a tax expert with Martin and Associates, in Washington, D.C., says, "First-time buyers should definitely work with a local tax preparer who has knowledge of all first-time homebuyer incentives and tax credits to be sure they take full advantage of them. These programs need to be researched because they each have different rules, so it's best to work with someone who can do that research for you. Best of all would be to go to a tax preparer or accountant before buying so these credits can be calculated into your preparations for buying a home."

First-time buyers like Barbara and Bob may be eager to ease their cash flow by adjusting their withholding allowances, but everyone needs to be very cautious when doing this. If you underestimate the allowances taken, you will get a tax refund. But if you take an extreme approach and have too little withheld, you may end up with a substantial tax bill. The IRS Form W-4 includes a worksheet that is helpful in determining the allowances to take, which will result in an appropriate amount of taxes withheld.

The more exemptions you take, the more money you keep as take-home pay because the IRS assumption is that you will need that money to pay for your expenses. If you lower your exemptions, more money will be withheld in taxes. You can even have zero exemptions or allowances withheld if you are concerned that you may owe taxes and want to make sure enough taxes are withheld each month.

In order to avoid miscalculating how buying a home may impact your taxes, Martin recommends that first-time buyers recalculate the previous year's taxes based on the purchase of a home before making any change to estimated tax payments or withholding.

"In most cases people will be able to reduce their withholding, which can help them make their monthly payments," says Martin. "First-time buyers usually will have been using a standard deduction, so making the switch to itemized deductions could potentially have a big impact on their taxes. Basically, they just need to run a tax return. Even the previous year's return will give a good approximation of the taxes due, unless there's a major change in income. Buyers can pick up Turbotax or some other software to run the numbers, then go to their employer and make the change. They should make sure to do this for the state income tax, too, because most states accept pretty much the same deductions as the federal income tax."

First-time buyers who opt to do their taxes themselves rather than hire a tax preparer should also make sure that itemizing deductions will give them the largest possible deduction. In some cases, the standard deduction may be higher and should be used. This would be especially true for buyers who purchased a home late in the year and therefore have only one or two months of mortgage interest and property taxes to deduct.

Martin says, "Another option, which is new for 2009, is that even consumers who use the standard deduction can take an extra $500 as a real estate tax deduction, or $1,000 for a couple filing jointly. For those who normally do the standard deduction, this might make sense since the standard deduction has been raised. They should run the numbers both ways to see if this makes sense. This especially works for people who have paid cash for a house or inherited a house and don't have any mortgage interest to deduct."

Mortgage interest typically represents the largest dollar amount of the tax deduction. First-time buyers should realize that even if they have opted for seller financing or they have borrowed money from a relative to buy a home, they may be able to deduct the interest paid on these loans. As long as the individuals who have loaned the money to buy the house are charging interest and documenting the payments, the borrowers can deduct the interest paid. Consulting a real estate lawyer and a tax expert would be wise in this situation to make sure that all the paperwork is completed accurately.

First-time buyers will need to keep all the paperwork from their settlement in a safe location along with other tax-related papers. Particularly important is the "HUD-1" statement, which lists every item paid at the settlement table.

Martin says that first-time buyers should look for Form 1098 from their lender, which will tell them how much they have paid in mortgage interest. This form usually arrives by February 1st. In some cases, not all the mortgage interest paid appears on the 1098 form because some of the mortgage interest will have been paid separately at the settlement. Be sure to compare the HUD-1 form and the 1098 form for accuracy.

If the buyers have opted to have the mortgage company pay their real estate taxes, then these taxes will show up on the 1098 form. If the buyers have opted to pay their real estate taxes separately, then they need to have their cancelled checks and receipts to make sure they properly deduct those taxes from their federal income taxes.

As long as the home you have bought is your principal residence, the points paid at the settlement table are fully tax deductible in the year you purchased the home. Points are listed on the HUD-1 form on lines 801 and 802. Sometimes they are labeled "points," but in different areas of the country or by different lenders they can also be labeled "loan origination fees" or "loan discounts." So, for example, if you paid two points to lower your mortgage interest rate on a $200,000 mortgage, you would have paid $4,000 at the settlement. In some cases, buyers are able to negotiate with the sellers to have them pay these points. Even if that is the case, the buyers are usually allowed to deduct the points paid at settlement.

In some cases, buyers who pay private mortgage insurance may be able to deduct those payments from their taxes, too. This varies depending on the household income. For 2008, mortgage insurance premiums are deductible for households filing jointly with an income of under $109,000. The deduction is partially phased out for those households with an income between $100,000 and $109,000.

While mortgage interest payments, property taxes, and points (and sometimes mortgage insurance premiums) are deductible, other expenses associated with homeownership are not deductible. In particular, homeowners cannot deduct their principal payments, homeowners insurance premiums, and homeowner or condominium association fees.

As first-time buyers are reviewing their HUD-1 settlement sheet, they may notice some other fees and taxes in addition to property taxes and assume they can deduct these, too. For example, appraisal, credit report, and administrative fees will all be listed on the HUD-1 form, but they are not tax-deductible expenses. States also charge taxes—which are variously called "stamp taxes," "recordation fees," or "transfer taxes"—but these are considered administrative fees even though they are collected by the state and local government, so these are not tax deductible.

First-time buyers are rarely thinking about selling their home, but they should be preparing for that eventuality throughout the time they own a property. When it comes time to sell, homeowners will need a copy of the original HUD-1 statement or at least a record of what they paid for the house when it was purchased. In addition, homeowners should be keeping a folder that documents any permanent type of repairs or improvements to the property, including new appliances, heating and air conditioning systems, a new roof, and things like driveway resurfacing and landscaping. There may be tax consequences for these home improvements during the period of ownership or at the time of sale. In particular, homeowners should keep track of any home improvements that add to the energy efficiency of the residence because there are often state and federal government tax deductions available for these types of projects.

Tax Resources

- For assistance in finding a tax consultant or preparer, visit the National Association of Enrolled Agents, NAEA.org. Specialists are certified by the Internal Revenue Service and can be located by zip code.

- The Internal Revenue Service website, IRS.gov, includes downloadable publications that provide information on tax laws.

- Publication 530: Tax Information for First-time Homeowners

- Publication 936: The Home Mortgage Interest Deduction

Understanding Your Contract

In addition to the tax consequences of buying a home, first-time buyers should be sure they understand everything they're signing when purchasing a home. An experienced agent should explain every document before it's signed and what the signed document means for you legally. Most Realtors work on a daily basis with a standard purchase agreement for their state.

Lenders should also be able to explain every line of the financial documents you will sign in order to apply for a loan.

When you don't understand something, stop before signing and ask for an explanation. But if at any time you're not satisfied with the answer given by your real estate agent or your lender, it's reasonable to ask a real estate lawyer for assistance.

Jim Savitz, a real estate attorney with Village Settlements in Gaithersburg, Maryland, says, "Do read all the paperwork before you sign a contract and make sure you understand it, or at the very least, get good advice from a lawyer or Realtor. Particularly pay attention to clauses related to property condition issues, especially if you're buying a foreclosure. For example, if the owner is in the property, then their first priority won't be taking care of the property. No one will pay to fix up the place, either, if the property is bank-owned, so the buyers need to make sure they factor fix-up costs into the price of the home."

It's important to understand standard purchase contracts from the beginning of the home-buying process because this document will determine the final outcome for the sellers and for the buyers. Some elements of the contract, such as whether certain items convey with the property, could have a lasting financial impact on the buyers, particularly if they need to purchase a number of major appliances.

Homeowners and Condominium Associations

Buying a condominium, co-op, or home located within the jurisdiction of a homeowners association will also have an impact on the homebuyers, either financially or as a lifestyle issue.

Ralph McMillan, a real estate attorney with McMillan-Terry, in Charlotte, North Carolina, says, "On the financial side, it's important to check out the association fees and how much they could go up. In a new community, the builders often control the fees while the development is under construction.

It's important to know how much they can go up after the builder pulls out so you are prepared to pay them."

Savitz says buyers need to look at the costs and expenses of any associations.

"Buyers should especially make sure to check into whether a special assessment is coming up," says Savitz. "Buyers should look at the budget to see if the association has some reserves."

McMillan says that before finalizing a purchase, buyers should review all homeowners association and condominium documents carefully. Most states have a "review period" for these documents, which allows the potential buyers to be released from the contract if they find something they don't want to live with. In Virginia, for example, buyers in a homeowners association or a condominium have three days from the day they receive the documents to look them over and pull out of the contract and have their deposit returned if they are not satisfied with the association's rules or finances.

"Buyers need to be really careful to review the association documents for architectural and neighborhood controls," says McMillan. "For instance, some communities won't allow you to have a boat or an RV on the premises. You need to find out before you buy whether you can add an addition, paint the house a different color, or add a fence."

The most important thing for buyers in a homeowners or condominium association is to determine what they want to do with their property and to make sure they won't be restricted.

"Buyers need to think about the way they live and whether it will be impacted by association rules," says Savitz. "For instance, can they put up a ham radio tower? Will there be a restriction against offering childcare in the home or operating another type of home business?"

Even businesses that are not necessarily conducted in the home, but require certain equipment, can be affected by homeowner association rules. For example, a contractor may not be allowed to park his pick-up truck on the street in some communities with rules about the types of vehicles allowed on the premises. Businesses that generate traffic either through a high level of package or supply deliveries or through a larger number of customers coming and going may be banned by association rules. Doctors or consultants who intend to meet with clients in a home office need to make sure the association rules allow a regular stream of customers into the community.

On the positive side, homeowner association rules can sometimes work in your favor. If your neighbors consistently leave trash outside, allow the exterior of their home to fall into disrepair, or park an unusable, abandoned car in the driveway for months on end, your homeowners association may be able to enforce rules that can put a stop to these actions. This is especially important later on when you want to sell your home, since the neighborhood appearance clearly affects the value of your home.

Savitz says buyers should be particularly aware of any issues with the home not following the association rules even before they buy it. For example, if the owner has put up a nonconforming fence, then the buyer should negotiate to have the seller pay the fine or fix the fence before they buy the place. Other concerns that could be expensive for the buyer to fix include removing an illegal hot tub from a back yard or repainting the exterior of the home to match the required color palette of a community.

Holding Title: Buying with a Spouse, Relatives, or Friends

Far more important than paint colors or hot tubs, though, is the issue of how to arrange the ownership of a home in legal terms. The legality of how owners hold title to a property varies from state to state and is an especially important consideration for unmarried homeowners.

"It's pretty simple if you are married—you normally own the property jointly so that if anything happens to one spouse the property automatically goes to the other," says McMillan. "In some states this is called 'tenants by entirety,' in others it is 'joint tenants with right of survivorship.'"

McMillan says that most people will own a home as joint tenants even if they are not married, as long as they want the property to automatically revert to the other owner if something happens to them. This works for couples buying a home together as well as unmarried relatives such as a brother and sister or mother and daughter.

A more complex scenario takes place when friends decide to buy a home together. Sometimes friends want the advantage of a great bargain property, such as a foreclosure, for investment purposes and then live in it for a certain period of time. Other times friends choose to buy just so they have the tax and potential investment benefits of homeownership while not carrying the entire financial burden themselves.

"In the case of friends buying together, they may want to own as "tenants in common," in which case the property is passed on by way of a will to the heirs of the owners, not to the other owner," says McMillan. "But in the case of friends buying together, there needs to be some sort of legal agreement about how the ownership would evolve, especially if one wants to move before the other owners do. I'd recommend consulting a lawyer with real estate experience and also estate matters, not just a title attorney, in the case of friends buying together, because this is much more complicated than standard homeownership."

✓ **CHECKLIST**

❑ Save your HUD-1 settlement sheet in order to prepare your taxes.

❑ Before adjusting your withholding to improve cash flow, recalculate your previous year's taxes and/or fill out the W-4 worksheet to estimate your appropriate withholding.

❑ Consider consulting a tax expert before adjusting your take-home pay.

❑ Review IRS Publication 530 for tax information for first-time homebuyers.

❑ Continue to ask your real estate agent and your lender to explain every document you sign; if you don't understand something, hire a real estate lawyer to help you.

❑ Review all homeowners association and condominium association documents for financial statements; make sure you know what your association dues will be, how much they might go up in future years, and whether a special assessment might be necessary.

❑ Review all homeowner association and condominium association documents for rules and regulations that could impact you and your family, such as restrictions on childcare or other businesses, boat storage, and even paint colors.

❑ Carefully consider (and consult with a real estate attorney if necessary) how the title should be held on the property.

❑ If you are buying a home with one or more friends, consult a real estate attorney and perhaps an estate attorney to be sure all papers are drawn appropriately to protect all owners.

CHAPTER ELEVEN

What to Expect at the Settlement Table

When Kathy and David bought their first home, they could hardly wait for their settlement day. When they arrived with their real estate agent for their walk-through on the morning of their settlement day, they eagerly opened the front door and instantly noticed an odor of sour milk. Their Realtor turned to them and said, "Do you remember what I told you about a house having to be left 'broom clean'? Not everyone has the same idea of what that means."

To Kathy and David, "broom-clean" meant a sparkling clean bathroom, polished floors, a dust-free mantel, and a shining refrigerator both inside and out. As they worked their way through the house, they realized that the sellers of their new home definitely had lower standards. Although the kitchen shelves were empty, the counters were sprinkled with crumbs and a splash of milk was congealed on the top shelf of the refrigerator.

While disappointed, Kathy and David knew there was nothing they could do about the less-than-ideal condition of their new home but to come back and clean it before they moved in with their belongings. But they were more disappointed by the condition of the living-room fireplace. As part of the signed contract, they had asked the sellers to repair the fireplace, which had a long crack in the slate hearth. But the buyers and the sellers had signed a simple addendum that said that the seller had to repair the crack. The sellers had used a do-it-yourself repair kit, which left the hearth crack only slightly less visible. They could have written the addendum to read, "seller to professionally repair and provide receipts," which would have left them with some recourse at the settlement table if they weren't satisfied. Instead, Kathy and David needed to repair the hearth on their own after they moved into their new home.

While plenty of Realtors can share settlement-day horror stories, the truth is that most settlements proceed smoothly. The best way to make sure that the settlement goes well is to carefully follow all the steps leading up to the closing. A good lender and a good Realtor will have prepared the buyers so that nothing should be surprising on the settlement date, even in these trying times. The key is to stay in close touch with both your agent and your lender to make sure there are no unexpected problems, particularly with the loan.

The most common settlement problems occur when the financing falls through for the buyers. This is one reason real estate agents recommend against choosing a lender through the Internet. When buyers work with a local lender, one well-known to the real estate agent, the chances are higher that even if glitches occur, the lender can find a way to fix them. A local lender, especially one well-connected within the local real estate community, will be more likely to aggressively resolve issues.

Choosing a Settlement Company

In most real estate transactions, the buyers are the ones to choose the settlement company. While it may seem like a long time between the day your contract is accepted by the sellers and the closing date or settlement date, buyers should choose a settlement company (also known as a title company) as soon as the contract is ratified. A ratified contract is simply one that has been agreed on and signed by both the buyers and the sellers.

Real estate agents will normally recommend a title company to the buyers. Since agents attend countless settlements each year, an experienced agent should be able to recommend a company that is consistently reliable in their service.

Ralph McMillan, a real estate attorney with McMillan-Terry, in Charlotte, North Carolina, says, "One thing that has changed a lot in the settlement process in recent years is how much more complex it is. It used to be one hour to do a simple settlement, and now it takes much longer just to explain the nuances of the papers that need to be signed and to absorb the information on all the material."

McMillan says that the important thing for buyers is to have a competent title agent or attorney (laws vary by state on who actually does the settlement)—a professional who will be there when something goes wrong. Some settlement companies have been going out of business as the market slows, so hopefully there are fewer incompetent companies around. One benefit of the slower housing market is that fewer "fly-by-night" lenders and settlement companies are in business.

"Buyers need to rely on their Realtor to recommend a professional settlement attorney, so the important thing is to pick a qualified Realtor in the first place who is careful and concerned about the buyer's benefits," says McMillan.

What to Expect Before the Settlement Day

Federal law requires lenders to provide a "Good Faith Estimate" of the fees you will pay at the settlement within three days of applying for a loan. You and your lender should review this estimate as soon as you receive it, especially if you have any questions about the document or any fees. The U.S. Department of Housing and Urban Development (HUD) developed a new, shorter form for the Good Faith Estimate, which all lenders must begin using by January 1, 2010. This form includes an instruction sheet to help borrowers understand the terms of their loan, including the length of the loan, whether the interest rate is fixed or adjustable, whether there is a prepayment penalty or a balloon payment. In addition, this statement will have an estimate of all closing costs. Understanding this form will go a long way to making the settlement day easier.

While you are reviewing this document and arranging for utilities to be turned on and the bills transferred to your name, arranging for a mover, and making sure you have a paid receipt for your homeowners insurance, the settlement company will be requesting a title report or title abstract from the county government where your new home is located. This report looks at the history of ownership of the property and investigates whether there are any outstanding liens, judgments, or lawsuits against the property. (Liens such as a mortgage or a home equity loan will be paid at settlement.) The title report determines whether you will be able to purchase the home and whether you can insure it.

At the same time as the title report is being researched, a house location survey will be ordered. This property survey is done to make sure there are no problems with things like fences being located on a neighbor's property or a neighbor's fence on your property. The house location survey will also look at whether any part of the house or anything else such as a shed or garage has been built over the property lines. A house location survey does not need to be done for condominiums.

Once the house location survey and the title report have been done, the settlement company will prepare the title insurance policy, which covers the lender. At the same time, buyers should request their own title insurance. Most settlement companies will automatically offer it to buyers, and Realtors will remind their buyers of the wisdom of purchasing this, but buyers should also be aware of the possibility of purchasing this protection.

It's a good idea to check in with a contact at the title company a week or so before the settlement date to make sure everything is in order and that there are no problems that you need to resolve before the closing.

The Walk-Through

After you have signed the contract and all the addendums to the contract that may have been added after the home inspection, you and the sellers then agree to the items that will convey and agree that the home will be left in good condition, or at least in the same condition as when it was inspected. In order to determine whether everything has been done in accordance with the contract, the buyers need to do a "walk-through" inspection either on the settlement date or as close as possible to that date.

In some cases, the sellers will not have moved all of their belongings from the house. If that is the case, then the buyers and sellers will have agreed to a "lease-back" arrangement so that the sellers are actually renting the house from the buyers after the settlement, when the buyers become the legal owners of the property. If no such arrangement has been made, then the sellers should have moved everything out of the house by the time of the walk-through.

While the walk-through can be an exciting moment because you are seeing again what will be your new home, possibly for the first time in weeks since the date of the home inspection, it is very important to be logical and meticulous in your inspection of the house. Pay particular attention to the items specified in the contract that were to convey to the buyers. If anything is missing, you will need to bring this to the attention of the sellers and their agent at the settlement to have the items replaced or to ask for compensation for the items.

It's also vital to check on the status of any repairs requested after the home inspection. If the sellers didn't have something repaired, they need to agree in writing to pay for the repairs when you have them done at a later date.

If you find something wrong with the home that was not covered in the contract, you should consult with your Realtor to see if this is something that should be discussed at the settlement. If a home inspector missed a problem that could be expensive to fix, it may be worth it to ask for compensation at the settlement table. Your Realtor should be able to give you advice as to how best to handle such a situation.

Just remember that a minor problem, while frustrating, may not be worth bringing up at the settlement. Asking the sellers to fix something just as they have vacated the property and are presumably eager to settle into their new home could create an extremely emotional reaction on their part, especially if they feel they have sold their home for less than what it is worth and that you got a bargain. Settlements have been delayed or derailed because the buyers want the sellers to fix an item that could cost $200 to replace. Think carefully about how little something may cost to handle on your own compared with the thousands you are committing to spending to buy the home you (hopefully) love.

While the majority of settlements go smoothly, you should realize the potentially significant financial consequences of a settlement that cannot be completed. In every case, the reason for the transaction not going to settlement will determine what happens to the money that has been committed up to this point. If you, as the buyer, suddenly get cold feet and decide you just don't want to buy the property, you are likely to forfeit your earnest money deposit. If a significant flaw in the home has been found at the walk-through, such as all the kitchen cabinets and appliances have been removed or a hole in the roof was discovered, then you need to negotiate with the seller and the seller's agent to have repairs or reparations made. If the seller will not cooperate and the sale cannot go through, then the buyer in this case is likely to have the earnest money deposit returned, since the problem is being created by the seller. In less clear-cut cases, the deposit will be held until the dispute can be resolved through negotiations, mediation, or in the worst case scenario, the legal system.

What to Expect at the Settlement

After the walk-through inspection, buyers should be ready to go to the settlement. In preparation for the closing, your lender and the settlement company should be in communication to make sure the loan documents are ready in time. If you have any doubts about whether they are working together or any other issue in preparation for the settlement, you should contact either the title company or the lender or both.

Each buyer who will be signing the paperwork needs to bring photo identification. In addition, the buyers need to bring the cash for closing in certified funds, either a cashier's check or a certified check made out to the title company. Buyers should contact the settlement company to find out exactly how much is needed in certified funds. In addition, you should bring a checkbook in case you need a small amount of additional funds at the last minute. You will also need to bring the documentation for your homeowners insurance to the closing, unless this has already been provided directly to the lender or to the settlement company by the insurance company.

If you're purchasing a foreclosure, you should be prepared for a more complex settlement.

Jim Savitz, a real estate attorney with Village Settlements, in Gaithersburg, Maryland, says, "Over 50% of the deals we see at the settlement table now are bank-owned foreclosures, which present a different set of challenges. The banks are usually not local and are usually represented by an asset manager who is afraid of losing his job. This means the bank will be very cautious and very slow in responding to anything. Often settlements today are more complicated because of last-minute financing and title problems, especially with foreclosures. For instance, there will have been improper notice of the foreclosure to subordinate lien holders on the property, with the second-trust loan not wiped out yet by the foreclosure."

The only way a buyer can be prepared for a challenging settlement is to work with experienced, professional lenders, real estate agents, and settlement attorneys who can work together to resolve any issues.

Closing costs are typically 3 to 5% of the price of the home, and some of these fees are paid by the buyer. Buyers should expect to pay charges from the lender, including loan origination fees, and document and processing fees.

Because settlements cannot always occur on the first or last day of the month, buyers need to pay pro-rated expenses at the settlement. For example, buyers normally pay the interest charges on the mortgage from the closing date until the end of the month. An escrow account is normally established with homeowners insurance and property taxes to be held in reserve so they are available when the first bills come in.

The title company charges are next, which include fees for a title search and examination, plus title insurance. Government recording and transfer charges are also paid by the buyer, and often there are additional settlement charges for items such as a termite inspection, survey, and mailing fees.

At the settlement, buyers should be sure to check the actual fees against the Good Faith Estimate for items such as processing fees or underwriting fees, notary fees, and courier or overnight delivery fees. These are all standard charges, but if they seem excessively high, buyers should question their settlement agent to find out why.

Settlement Documents

One of the more frightening aspects of the settlement is the mountain of papers signed, but you actually will have seen most of these papers before the closing. Many of the papers to sign are simply repeats of things such as your loan application, which you are signing again to verify that nothing has changed in your employment, marital, or financial status since you originally provided this information.

Other papers include a declaration that you will be occupying the property (in other words, that you are not an investor, which has different requirements) and that your legal mailing address will be your new home.

There are four documents at the closing that are the most important to review and understand.

1. **The HUD-1 Settlement Statement:** This should be the first document you see and sign at the closing. On this sheet, the buyers' charges and credits are listed on the left side of the page, and the sellers' charges and credits are listed on the right side of the page.

2. **The Truth-in-Lending Statement:** This disclosure is mandatory under federal law and gives the borrowers an estimate of the annual cost of their mortgage loan over the full term of the loan, factoring in all the costs and fees you are paying.

The Annual Percentage Rate (APR) listed here may not be the same as the interest rate you are paying because it's based on the actual loan amount and your proposed payments. The APR is often slightly higher than the interest rate on your loan. The Truth-in-Lending Statement should also tell you whether or not any late fee will be assessed for a late payment and whether any penalty exists for prepayment of your loan.

3. **Promissory Note:** Review this note to be sure that the interest rate, the loan amount, and the loan term are correct. The Note should state whether there is a prepayment penalty for the loan, and it should state that the late charge for a late payment should not exceed 5% of your past due principal and interest. The Note may also disclose whether your loan is assumable or not. If not, a future purchaser of your home won't be able to take over your payments. That purchaser will have to obtain their own loan.

4. **Deed of Trust:** Signing this document means that you are pledging the house as collateral against the mortgage loan. If you default on the loan, this is the document that allows the lender to foreclose on the property.

Once all the papers have been signed, the buyers are ready to receive the keys to their new home. While it is certainly not a requirement, it's helpful if the sellers will also leave in the home any manuals for working the appliances. Carry-out menus from local restaurants, a list of the local veterinarians and babysitters might be nice, too. Even better, a bottle of champagne in the refrigerator to welcome you, the new homeowners.

✓ CHECKLIST

❑ Choose a settlement company recommended by your Realtor as soon as the contract has been accepted by the sellers and a settlement date has been agreed to.

❑ Review the Good Faith Estimate from your lender.

❑ Arrange for utilities to be transferred to your name and connected on the settlement day.

❑ Arrange for a moving company early. During busy months and on weekends at the end of the month, they can be booked quickly.

❑ Arrange for your mail and newspaper deliveries to begin after your settlement date.

❑ Make sure you have arranged for homeowners insurance and that the receipt for this insurance arrives in your hands or with the lender or title company before the settlement date.

❑ Stay in touch with your lender, Realtor, and the title company, especially as the settlement date approaches to make sure all documents are ready and no problems have occurred.

❑ Arrange with your Realtor for a walk-through inspection of your new home on the settlement date or just before it.

❑ Pay close attention during the walk-through to the items that were supposed to convey with the property, anything the sellers were to repair or replace, and to the overall condition of the home, which should be the same as when you last inspected it.

(continued on next page)

✓ **CHECKLIST**

(continued from previous page)

❏ Consult with your Realtor if there are any issues discovered at the walk-through. A minor problem may not be worth bringing up since it can delay or cancel the settlement.

❏ All buyers need to bring photo identification to the closing, along with the proof of their homeowners insurance if it has not already been delivered to the settlement company.

❏ The cash you need to close (closing costs and down payment minus your earnest money deposit) must be in certified funds. Bring a checkbook, too, in case the estimate given to you by the settlement company is slightly off.

❏ Compare your HUD-1 Settlement Statement with your Good Faith Estimate. If there's a major difference in a fee or something you don't understand, ask about it. Sometimes someone simply made a mistake on the form and you don't want to pay extra for that mistake.

❏ Make sure you understand each paper before you sign it. If you don't understand something, ask for it to be explained. You are spending a lot of money and the settlement company is earning a lot of money for their services, so you should use them.

❏ *Pat yourself on the back—you've bought your first home!*

Glossary of Real Estate Terms

Addendum: An addition to the standard contract, covering specific items such as asking for certain items to convey to the buyers.

Adjustable-Rate Mortgage (ARM): A mortgage loan with an interest rate that periodically changes in response to the market or to Treasury Bill rates.

Amendment: A change to the contract to add new information or alter a previous section of the contract.

Amortize: Paying off the mortgage debt through regular installment payments of both principal and interest over a set period of time, making equal or nearly equal payments until the loan is paid.

Annual Percentage Rate (APR): The yearly interest rate paid on a loan. Federal law requires that this rate is disclosed as part of the truth-in-lending documents.

Appraisal: An estimate of the value of the property by a professional appraiser.

Assumable Mortgage: A mortgage loan that can be transferred from one owner of a property to the new owner.

Balloon Mortgage: A mortgage loan with an initially low interest rate and low payments for a certain period of time with one large payment due at the end of that period.

Buy-Down Mortgage: A mortgage loan for which the buyers, the sellers, a third party, or even the lender pays an initial lump sum to lower the interest rate for a set period of time (usually one to five years) in order to reduce the initial monthly payments.

Closing: Also called the "settlement" when all papers are signed and the ownership of the property transfers from one owner to the next.

Commission: The fee paid to the buyer's agent and the seller's agent from the proceeds of the sale of the home.

Comparable Sales (Comps): Sales prices of similar properties used to estimate the market value of the property by Realtors and appraisers.

Contingency: A part of the contract that states the contract will be null and void and the deposit returned if the stated conditions are not met; for example, many contracts are contingent on a satisfactory home inspection and on the buyer obtaining financing based on the appraisal.

Conventional Mortgage: A mortgage offered by a lender, which is likely to be purchased on the secondary loan market by Fannie Mae or Freddie Mac; these loans have an upper limit of $625,500.

Convertible ARM: An adjustable-rate loan that can be converted to a fixed-rate mortgage during a certain time period.

Credit Score: A number assigned by each of the three credit reporting agencies that reflects the credit history of the consumer and changes according to the current financial situation of the consumer; also known as a "FICO" score, a trademark of the Fair Isaac Corporation.

Deed: The legal document used to convey ownership to the titleholders.

Disclaimer: A legal form that's part of the contract in some states, allowing sellers to state that they have no knowledge of any defects in their property.

Disclosure: A legal form, which is part of the contract in some states, in which sellers need to disclose all their knowledge about property defects.

Down Payment: A cash portion of the payment for a property that's due at the settlement. Many conventional loans require a down payment of 10 to 20%; FHA loans require 3.5%; some VA loans are available with zero down payment.

Earnest Money Deposit: A deposit included with the initial contract offer for a home, often representing 1 to 5% of the offer amount, usually held in an escrow account until the settlement so it cannot be spent.

Equity: The amount of the property owned after all liabilities are subtracted from the market value of the property; also known as assets.

Escrow: An account held by the lender, which includes homeowner payments for taxes and homeowners insurance, until those bills are due; the earnest money deposit is also held in escrow until the settlement.

Fannie Mae: Government-sponsored organization that buys mortgages from lenders in order to make loans more available and affordable.

Federal Housing Administration: Government agency offering low down payment loans along with housing information.

Fixed-Rate Mortgage: A mortgage loan in which the interest rate remains the same for the entire length of the loan.

Foreclosure: The legal process that occurs when the borrowers have become delinquent on their loan and the lender repossesses the property and sells it. The proceeds of the sale are then applied to the mortgage debt.

Freddie Mac: Government-sponsored organization that buys mortgages from lenders in order to make loans more available and affordable.

Good Faith Estimate: An estimate of the entire cost of buying a home, including all down payment, interest payments, and closing costs associated with a loan; to be provided by the lender within three days of a loan application.

Hazard Insurance: Insurance that protects homeowners and lenders against financial loss from fire or other damages (same as homeowners insurance).

Home Equity Line of Credit: Homeowners can borrow money against the equity in their home to pay for things such as home improvements, college tuition or personal expenses; the amount available will vary according to the appraised value of the home versus the outstanding mortgage debt.

Home-Warranty Program: A program that provides insurance for repairing appliances and systems in the home for a limited time; often paid for by sellers to give buyers extra protection during their first year of homeownership.

Homeowners Association: An association to which homeowners are required to belong if they own a home within the boundaries of the association; members must pay dues and follow the rules of the association.

Homeowners Insurance: Insurance protecting homeowners and lenders against financial loss from fire or other damages (same as hazard insurance).

Interest-only Mortgage: A mortgage that allows the borrowers to pay just the interest on the loan for a certain set time period; at the end of that time, the loan payments will go up and include the principal payments.

Jumbo Loan: Any mortgage loan above $625,500; these loans often carry a higher interest rate and will require a higher down payment and higher credit score than smaller loans.

Lease-Option or Lease-Purchase: A legal agreement between a renter and a landlord, which establishes a protocol for allowing the renter to buy the property; agreements vary in whether the renter is obligated to buy or has an option to buy, the length of the agreement, and whether part of the rent is credited toward a purchase.

Loan Origination Fee: A fee charged by the lender for administering and processing the loan; also sometimes called a "point," equal to 1% of the loan amount.

Loan-to-Value: The amount of the mortgage loan in comparison to the value of the home; the difference between the two numbers represents the amount of equity the owner has in the home.

Mortgage Insurance: Insurance protecting the lender against loss if the borrower defaults on the loan.

Negative Amortization: A type of loan in which the borrower's payments are too low to cover all the interest owed and covers none of the principal; the balance due on the loan increases over time and is added to the principal.

Points: A fee charged by the lender equal to 1% of the loan amount; points can be paid at the closing to lower the interest rate on a loan.

Preapproval: An estimate of your ability to qualify for a loan given by a lender based on your credit worthiness, income, and assets but without a complete proof of all assets.

Prepayment Penalty: A payment required on some loans if the loan is paid in full before the end of the loan term by making extra payments, refinancing, or selling the property.

Prequalification: A qualification for a mortgage by a lender based on proof of your income, assets, and credit score, which states the maximum loan that you can qualify for; final loan approval also requires an appraisal on the property demonstrating that the value of the property is more than the loan amount.

Ratified Contract: A contract that has been signed and accepted by both the buyers and the sellers and their agents.

Recording Fees: Fees paid to the county or state for recording property ownership in land records.

RESPA (Real Estate Settlement Procedures Act): A consumer-protection act administered by the U.S. Department of Housing and Urban Development (HUD), which establishes rules for informing consumers about closing costs, settlement fees, and mortgage loans.

Rural Development Loans: Administered by the U.S. Department of Agriculture (rurdev.usda.gov); 100% financing loans with low interest rates; they are restricted to properties in designated rural areas, income limits may apply.

Seller Financing: In rare cases, home sellers are willing to arrange for all or part of the home purchase to be directly financed by them, usually when the home is an estate sale or the sellers own the home free and clear without a mortgage.

Settlement: The process during which buyers and sellers sign legal binding paperwork and loan documents that transfer the ownership of the property; also known as a "closing"; the buyers typically choose the settlement company; the settlement date is negotiable between the two sides of the transaction.

Settlement/Closing Fees: Fees charged by the settlement company for the processing of papers, examination of the title, and review of loan documents.

Short Sale: A sale of property when the home has a market value of less than the sellers owe on their mortgage loan; a short-sale agreement must be signed by the seller's lenders and the seller; the offer price must be agreed on by the seller, the lender, and the buyer.

Stamp Tax: In some states and counties, this is the name for the tax charged when property is transferred from one owner to another (also known as a transfer tax).

Survey: A professional, physical survey of the land being sold to determine the legal boundaries of the property and to review whether any encroachments have been made on the land; required before the title will be transferred and title insurance issued.

Title: The document that proves ownership of property.

Title Defect: Anything in the history of the ownership of a property that may create a problem for the owner's rights to some part of the property or the entire property.

Title Insurance: Insurance which protects the lender against title defects, usually required by lenders. Homebuyers can also buy their own title insurance to protect themselves in case of a title defect.

Transfer Tax: A tax, also known as a stamp tax, charged by the state or county government when property is transferred. The tax is part of the closing costs paid at settlement.

Truth-in-Lending: A statement required by the federal government to be presented to borrowers at the settlement, which discloses an estimate of the annual cost of the mortgage and the total cost of the loan over the loan's full term.

Veterans Administration (VA): A federal government agency which, among other benefits, guarantees mortgage loans for veterans, and members of the military and their families with lower interest rates and a low or zero down payment.

About State Housing Finance Programs

Most state housing finance programs have the following in common:

First Mortgages at Lower Rates:

Most housing finance agencies or authorities are self-supporting state agencies. Low-interest rate loans are made available through the sale of tax-exempt bonds (Mortgage Revenue Bonds). The bonds are repaid by revenues generated through mortgage loans, not taxpayer dollars. Prospective homebuyers are responsible for contacting approved lenders. These are listed on the state housing agency's website or can be accessed by calling the agency. The lender then determines if the prospective homebuyer qualifies for a loan based on FHA, VA, Rural Housing Service (RHS), or Conventional (Fannie Mae or Freddie Mac) loan standards.

Down Payment and/or Closing Cost Assistance:

Assistance can come in many forms, including second mortgages to be paid in conjunction with a first mortgage; no-interest fifteen-year second mortgages; deferred payment loans with no interest and no monthly payments, to be repaid on the sale or refinance of the home; or in the form of outright grants, which do not need to be repaid.

Mortgage Credit Certificates

This program offers the first-time homebuyer a federal income tax credit, which reduces the amount of federal taxes the holder of the certificate would pay. The qualified homebuyer may take an annual credit against the federal income taxes paid on their mortgage. The credit is subtracted dollar for dollar from the homebuyer's federal income taxes. The qualified buyer is awarded a tax credit of up to 15%, and the remaining 85% is taken as a deduction from the income in the usual manner.

Habitat for Humanity (or Other Nonprofit Agencies) Loan Purchase Programs:

These programs offer the possibility of homeownership to those willing and able to put several hundred hours of "sweat equity" into building a home, thereby reducing the purchase price. (Sweat equity is the interest in a building that a tenant earns by contributing to its construction, renovation, or maintenance.) The programs often include job-loss protection where the mortgage will be paid for six months in the case of involuntary unemployment, as well as assistance with mortgage payment, down payment, and closing costs.

Section 8 Homeownership:

A program for low-income recipients of rental assistance, where rental vouchers may be converted to homeownership vouchers upon the purchase of a home. Some of the requirements are that the purchaser must be a first-time homebuyer and meet minimum income and employment requirements, as well as meet any other eligibility requirements as stipulated by the local housing agency. Other forms of assistance in conjunction with the program are often available.

First-Time Homebuyer Requirement:

Most state programs are aimed at assisting first-time home-buyers. The law defines a first-time homebuyer as a buyer who has not owned a principal residence during the three-year period prior to the purchase. For married taxpayers, the law tests the homeownership history of both the homebuyer and his/her spouse. Ownership of a vacation home or rental property not used as a principal residence does not disqualify a buyer as a first-time buyer. However, in most cases, the buyer must use the home purchased through a state program as the primary residence. Unless otherwise specified, the programs in the following appendix are for first-time homebuyers.

Income Restrictions:

Most programs require that the homebuyer's income be below that of the AMI, Area Median Income. Often the amount is set at equal to or less than 80% of AMI. Income restrictions can vary from state to state and program to program.

Purchase Price Restrictions:

Most programs set purchase price restrictions by county. In some cases, target areas are set by the U.S. Census Bureau to encourage economic growth. Generally, purchases in target areas will be less restrictive in terms of income, purchase price, and prior homeownership. One can buy a slightly larger home or have a slightly higher income and still participate in various state-run programs. Purchases in a non-targeted area will have more stringent restrictions.

Recapture Tax:

This is a tax that the borrower may have to pay if the home is sold or transferred. Borrowers of tax-exempt financing receive the benefit of below-market interest rates, considered an indirect subsidy. The federal government uses the recapture tax to recoup some of this subsidy from the gain, if any, on the sale or transfer of the home. However, not all sales or transfers are subject to recapture. First, a sale or transfer of the home must occur within nine years of the date of purchase. Second, a borrower's income must be above the Adjusted Qualifying Income limit as calculated by household size at the time the home is sold or transferred, and the Recapture Tax Notice must have been received at the closing. Third, a gain on the sale or transfer of the home must occur. If there is no gain there is no recapture tax.

Homebuyer Education Courses Requirements:

Most states require borrowers or recipients of assistance to complete a homebuyer education class. These classes are offered online, or in person, or both. Most classes include information on: the advantages and disadvantages of owning a home, the true "cost" of homeownership aside from commissions and fees; steps to take when shopping for a home; identification of people you will need to work with during a purchase; planning monetary goals and developing a spending/saving plan to meet those goals; understanding credit, credit ratings, and credit reports, common credit problems, how to solve credit problems and manage debt; protection from identity theft, rehabilitation scams, and predatory lending practices; and guidance through the entire mortgage search from descriptions of various lending institutions and loan categories to mortgage terminology.

State-by-State Guide to First-Time Homebuyer Programs

ALABAMA

AHFA – Alabama Housing Finance Authority, 2000 Interstate Park Dr., Suite 408, Montgomery, AL 36109; AHFA.com; 334-244-9200; 800-325-2432

First Step: Offers below-market fixed interest rates on thirty-year mortgages. AHFA may also provide a percentage of the home's sales price in down payment and closing cost aid, financed over a twenty-year term.

American Dream Downpayment Initiative (ADDI): Reduces out-of-pocket expenses for first-time homebuyers with lower incomes. Assistance is a $10,000, 0% interest, five-year, forgivable, subordinate mortgage, used to reduced the first mortgage loan's principal balance.

Habitat for Humanity Loan Purchase Program: Provides families in need with no-interest, no-down payment mortgages. Families must contribute "sweat equity" and make modest mortgage payments.

Step Up: Provides up to 100% financing to income-qualified buyers using FHA or Rural Development loans. Down payment funds are blended into the home mortgage. Not restricted to first-time homebuyers.

Mortgage Credit Certificates: Reduces the amount of federal income tax homeowners pay, giving them more available income to qualify for a mortgage loan. Available in conjunction with Step Up. Not restricted to first-time homebuyers.

ALASKA

AHFC – Alaska Housing Finance Corporation, 4300 Boniface Pkwy., Anchorage, AK 99504; AHFC.state.ak.us; 907-338-6100; 800-478-2432

Tax Exempt First-Time Homebuyer Program (TEP): Low-interest fixed-rate mortgage loans. Targeted areas or qualified veterans not subject to first-time homebuyer restrictions. Federal income tax credit to make payments more affordable.

Taxable First-Time Homebuyer Program: For those wishing to purchase a home that exceeds the cost limits of TEP, or whose income exceeds TEP income limits.

Veterans Mortgage Program: Low-interest fixed-rate mortgage loans for qualified veterans. Not restricted to first-time homebuyers. Interest rate preference also available in the form of an interest rate reduction on the loan.

Rural Owner Occupied Loan Program: Low-interest fixed-rate mortgage loans for purchase of owner-occupied properties located in "small communities."

Teachers and Health Care Professionals Housing Loan Program: No down payment, 100% financing, low-interest mortgage loans to teaching and health care professionals.

Interest Rate Reduction for Low-income Borrowers (IRRLIB): Interest-rate reductions on fixed-rate mortgage loans, up to the first $180,000 of the loan amount, rounded up gradually for amounts exceeding $180,000.

Affordable Housing Enhanced Loan Program (AHELP): Down-payment assistance as a grant, deferred payment, forgivable loan, or combination of the above.

Second Mortgage Program: Second mortgage loan under the Taxable or Rural Owner Occupied loan programs, to finance home improvements or purchase a home with an assumption and make repairs.

ARIZONA

AZHFA – Arizona Housing Finance Authority, 1110 W. Washington, Suite 310, Phoenix, AZ 85007 ; Housingaz.com/azhfa; 602-771-1000

Mortgage Revenue Bond (MRS) Home Loans for First-Time Buyers: Provides a thirty-year fixed-rate mortgage at below-market rates.

Mortgage Credit Certificate (MCC) Tax Benefits for First-Time Homebuyers: Reduces federal income tax in the form of a credit to provide housing assistance to low- and moderate-income families.

Down Payment Assistance Program: Down-payment and closing-cost assistance in varying amounts.

ARKANSAS

ADFA – Arkansas Development Finance Authority, 423 Main St., Suite 500, P.O. Box 8023, Little Rock, AR 72203-8023; Arkansas.gov/adfa/programs; 501-682-5974

Home to Own Program: Below-market fixed-interest rates for thirty-year mortgages.

American Dream Downpayment Initiative (ADDI): Provides funding to assist low-income buyers with the upfront costs of buying a home.

Down Payment Assistance (DPA) Program: Loans for down-payment and closing-cost assistance. Interest rate varies, ten-year amortization on the loan.

CALIFORNIA

CalHFA – California Housing Finance Agency, 1415 L Street, Suite 500, Sacramento, CA 95814; CalHFA.ca.gov; 877-922-5432

CalHFA Conventional Loans: Conventional mortgage loan offering up to 95% financing with a thirty-year term and a low, fixed-interest rate.

Government Insured/Guaranteed Loans: Mortgage loans insured or guaranteed by FHA, VA, or USDA, featuring a thirty-year term with a low, fixed-interest rate.

CalHFA Community Stabilization Home Loan Program: Helps first-time homebuyers purchase vacant homes that are owned by participating financial institutions in certain areas of California.

Affordable Housing Partnership Program (AHPP): Joint effort by CalHFA and localities offers a deferred payment subordinate loan to assist with down payment and closing costs.

California Homebuyer's Down Payment Assistance Program (CHDAP): Deferred payment junior loan of an amount up to the lesser of 3% of the purchase price or appraised value, to assist with down payment and closing costs.

Extra Credit Teacher Home Purchase Program (ECTP): Low-interest rate CalHFA First loan, combined with a forgivable interest CalHFA junior loan to assist eligible teachers, administrators, staff members, and classified employees to purchase their first home.

School Facility Fee Down Payment Assistance Program (SFF): Conditional grant program (based on a partial or full rebate of the school facility fees paid by the home builder) that provides assistance to buyers of newly constructed homes throughout California. Grant can be used for down payment or closing costs.

HomeOpeners, a Mortgage Protection Program: Helps borrowers pay their mortgage in the event of involuntary job loss. Offered as part of primary mortgage insurance at no additional cost to the borrower or lender.

HUD – Section 8 Housing Choice Voucher Program: Enables qualified first-time homebuyers to receive monthly assistance for homeownership expenses in lieu of monthly rent aid.

COLORADO

CHFA – Colorado Housing and Finance Authority, 1981 Blake St., Denver, Colorado 80202-1272; CHFAinfo.com; 303-297-2432; 800-877-2432

MRB First Step (Mortgage Revenue Bond)L: Affordable fixed-interest rate mortgage loan, optional second mortgage to assist with down payment and closing costs, and reimbursement for the full amount of Recapture Tax if the home is sold.

Taxable Home Opener: First mortgage program that accepts higher incomes than the MRB First Step, offers competitive interest rate and an optional second mortgage to assist with down payment and closing costs. Not restricted to first-time homebuyers.

CHFA HomeStretch: Forty-year fixed-interest conventional loan for acquisition or refinance of a home. Higher-income limits, no-purchase price limits, optional 0% interest rate second mortgage toward down payment and closing costs in amount up to 3% of first mortgage.

Second Mortgage Loans: In conjunction with MRB First Step or Taxable Home Opener, helps with down payment and closing costs. Thirty -year term, 0% interest rate, available for up to 3% of the first-mortgage loan amount.

HomeAccess Suite of Programs: First mortgages at below-market, fixed-interest rates for homebuyers with disabilities or a household member with a disability. HomeAccess Second Mortgage provides an optional $10,000 loan.

Mortgage Credit Certificate: Homebuyers may take a 20% credit against their federal income tax liability, and an 80% deduction for mortgage interest paid, using the savings toward their monthly mortgage payment. Only offered in targeted communities.

CONNECTICUT

CHFA – Connecticut Housing Finance Authority, 999 West St., Rocky Hill, CT 06067; CHFA.org; 860-721-9501

Homebuyer Mortgage Program: Thirty-year, fixed-rate loans at lower interest rates.

Down Payment Assistance Program (DAP): Used in conjunction with a CHFA first mortgage to provide assistance with down payments and closing costs.

HOYO: Thirty-year fixed-rate mortgages for persons with disabilities.

SmartMove Homeownership Fund Second Mortgage Program: Down-payment second-mortgage loan provided by the Housing Development. Fund in partnership with CHFA. Limited to targeted areas.

Homeownership Program (for residents of public housing): Thirty-year fixed-rate mortgages, restrictions on income and purchase price, required homebuyer education class to assist in preparing for the responsibilities of homeownership.

HUD – Section 8 Housing Choice Voucher Program: Enables qualified first-time homebuyers to receive monthly assistance for homeownership expenses in lieu of monthly rent aid.

Teachers Mortgage Assistance Program, Police Homeownership Program, Military Homeownership Program: These programs are available to first-time homebuyers in the indicated professions.

Rehabilitation Mortgage Loan Program/Pilot Urban Rehabilitation Homeownership (UR Home) Program: Funding is available for the purchase or refinance of a home in need of repair. Various restrictions apply, including targeted areas and state or municipal employment.

DELAWARE

DSHA – Delaware State Housing Authority, 18 The Green, Dover, DE 19901; DEstatehousing.com; 302-739-4263; 888-363-8808

Single Family Mortgage Revenue Bond Program (SFMRB): First mortgage financing at below-market interest rates for low- and moderate-income first-time homebuyers.

American Dream Down Payment Initiative (ADDI): Offers the greater of $10,000 or 6% of the sales contract price in down-payment assistance.

Resident Homeownership Program (RHP): Offers eligible DSHA assisted housing residents the option of purchasing a home using their existing assistance toward the mortgage.

Live Near Your Work (LNYW): Provides employees of participating employers with a grant toward the purchase of a home near their employment.

DISTRICT OF COLUMBIA

DCHFA – District of Columbia Housing Finance Agency, 815 Florida Ave., NW, Washington, DC 20001; DChfa.org; 202-777-1600

Single Family Mortgage Revenue Bond Program: Thirty-year fixed-rate low-interest mortgage loans.

DCHA– District of Columbia Housing Authority, 1133 North Capitol St., NE, Washington, DC 20001; DChousing.org; 202-535-1500

Housing Choice Voucher/Home Ownership Assistance Program/HOPE VI: Permits families with vouchers to use their subsidy benefits to purchase, occupy and own a home. Formerly Section 8.

DHCD – Department of Housing and Community Development, 801 North Capitol St., NE, 8th Floor, Washington, DC 20002; DHCD.dc.gov; 202-442-7200

Home Purchase Assistance Program: Interest-free and low-interest loans to help with down payment and closing costs.

Employer Assisted Housing Program: Assistance with down payment and closing costs for employees of the District of Columbia Government.

FLORIDA

FHFC – Florida Housing Finance Corporation, 227 N. Bronough St., Suite 5000, Tallahassee, FL 32301; FloridaHousing.org; 850-488-4197

First-Time Homebuyer Program: Offers fixed, low-interest-rate mortgage loans, as well as down-payment and closing-cost assistance to eligible low- to moderate-income families.

Homeownership Pool (HOP) Program: Developers become HOP Pool members and reserve funds for eligible homebuyers on a first-come, first-served basis.

Local Housing Programs (State Housing Initiatives Partnership – SHIP): Provides funds to local government as an incentive to create partnerships that produce and preserve affordable homeownership. Program designed to serve very low-, low-, and moderate-income families.

GEORGIA

DCA – Department of Community Affairs, 60 Executive Park South, NE, Atlanta, GA 30329-2231; DCA.state.ga.us; 404-679-4940; 800-359-4663

Georgia Dream Homeownership Program: Low-interest fixed-rate mortgage loans.

Georgia Dream Second Mortgage Standard: Loans in conjunction with Georgia Dream First Mortgage to help defray down-payments costs, closing costs, and prepaid items. These are delayed repayment second-mortgage loans that are repaid when the home is sold or refinanced. These loans are also available to specialized groups as follows:

PEN: Available to Protectors, Educators, and Health Care Workers.

EV: Available for homes certified as energy efficient.

CHOICE: Available for homeowners who are disabled or households with a disabled individual.

HONORS and WELCOME HOME: Available to members of the military or their surviving spouses.

HAWAII

HHFDC – Hawaii Housing Finance and Development Corporation, 677 Queen St., Honolulu, HI 96813; Hawaii.gov.dbedt/hhfdc; 808-587-0597

Hula Mae Program: Low-interest rates on mortgage loans for low- to moderate-income families.

Mortgage Credit Certificate Program: Reduces the amount of federal income tax paid, therefore giving the homeowner more available income to qualify for a mortgage loan and assist with house payments.

Down Payment Assistance Loan Program: Second-mortgage loan to assist with down payment and closing costs.

IDAHO

IHFA – Idaho Housing and Finance Association, 565 W. Myrtle, P.O. Box 7899, Boise, ID 83707-1899; IHFA.org; 208-331-4882; 866-432-4066

IdaMortgage Advantage Conventional: Below-market fixed-interest rates, no sales price limits, not limited to first-time homebuyers.

IdaMortgage First Loan Conventional: Low fixed-interest rate-mortgage loans.

IdaMortgage Advantage 40-Year Loan: Below-market fixed-rates, no sales price limits, not limited to first-time homebuyers.

Second Mortgage Program: Thirty-year fixed-interest second-mortgage loan to assist with down payment and closing costs.

HOME Down Payment Assistance Program: 0% deferred-payment loan program for assistance with down payment and closing costs. Loan becomes forgivable over time.

Good Credit Rewards: Second-mortgage program for assistance with down payment and closing costs. Interest rates are tiered by credit score and higher-income limits apply.

ILLINOIS

IHDA – Illinois Housing Development Authority, 401 North Michigan Ave., Suite 700, Chicago, IL 60611; IHDA.org; 312-836-5200

I-LOAN Mortgage (MRB) Program: Below-market interest rates for first-time homebuyers.

I-LOAN Certificate (Mortgage Credit Certificate – MCC): Direct credit on homebuyer's federal income tax for the life of the mortgage. Resulting higher income assists with mortgage payments and/or down payment and closing costs. (The two I-LOAN programs may not be combined.)

IHDA Affordable Housing Trust Fund: Down payment and closing cost assistance for low- and very low-income individuals. Funds are made available through organizations interested in expanding affordable housing.

Homebuyer Assistance/Rehabilitation Program: Down payment, closing cost and rehabilitation assistance to low-income homebuyers.

INDIANA

IHCDA – Indiana Housing and Community Development Authority, 30 South Meridian St., Suite 1000, Indianapolis, IN 46204; IN.gov/ihcda; 317-232-7777; 800-872-0371

First Home: Below-market fixed-interest-rate mortgages.

First Home/PLUS: First Home special mortgage rate, as well as 5% down-payment assistance. These funds must be repaid in full once the borrower sells or refinances the home.

First Home 100/Community Mortgage 100% Option: Partnership program with Fannie Mae offering affordable homeownership for low- to very low-income applicants. Flexible, with not as many qualifying standards, in order to assist a larger number of potential homeowners.

Community Solutions 100: Partnership program with Fannie Mae to allow teachers, firefighters, law enforcement, and state and municipal workers to buy a home with as little as $500 of their own money.

Community Home Choice: Partnership program with Fannie Mae that offers affordable homeownership opportunities for those with disabilities or a household member with disabilities.

Mortgage Credit Certificates: Offers first-time homebuyers a federal tax credit on mortgage interest, resulting in extra cash to help with mortgage, down payment, and/or closing costs.

Homeownership Program for Veterans: Low-interest fixed-mortgage rates. Not restricted to first-time homebuyers. However, first-time homebuyers may be entitled to extra down-payment assistance.

IOWA

IFA – Iowa Finance Authority, 2015 Grand Ave., Des Moines, IA 50312 ; IowaFinanceAuthority.gov; 515-725-4900; 800-432-7230

FirstHome Program: Low fixed-interest-rate mortgage loan. Targeted areas now include the eighty-six counties that have been declared federal disaster areas due to the 2008 storms and floods.

FirstHome Plus Program: Cash assistance to help with closing costs, down payments, or minor repairs.

Military Service Member Homeownership Assistance: Provides cash that may be used toward down payments and/or closing costs for eligible armed service members or their surviving spouses. Can be used in conjunction with FirstHome or FirstHome Plus.

Mortgage Credit Certificate: Federal income tax credit, resulting in extra cash to help with mortgage, down payment, or closing costs.

RuralHome Subsidy: Provides cash assistance for down payment and closing costs for first-time homebuyers who are purchasing homes in communities with a population under 25,000.

KANSAS

KHRC – Kansas Housing Resources Corporation, 611 South Kansas Ave., Suite 300, Topeka, KS 66603-3803; KShousingcorp.org; 785-296-5865

First-Time Homebuyers Program (FTHB): Down-payment assistance for the purchase of a first home.

Additional Programs: Most other programs available in Kansas provide assistance for homeowners to improve their homes for energy efficiency, general rehabilitation, disabled accessibility, emergency repairs, and weatherization.

KENTUCKY

KHC – Kentucky Housing Corporation, 1231 Louisville Road, Frankfort, Kentucky 40601-6191; KYhousing.org; 502-564-7630; 800-633-8896

Mortgage Revenue Bond (MRB) Loan Programs: Lower-interest fixed-rate mortgage loans.

Down Payment Assistance Programs for MRB Programs: These programs provide assistance for down payment, closing costs, and prepaid costs. Repayment terms depend on the type of program.

Regular Down Payment Assistance Program (DAP): Repaid over ten years at the same lower rate as the first mortgage loan.

HOME-DAP: No monthly repayment, forgiven over five years.

HOME Special Program: For households including a disabled person, or where one of the homebuyers is over age sixty-two. No monthly repayment, forgiven over five years.

HOME Family Program: For first-time homebuyer households where there is at least one dependent child. No monthly repayment, forgiven over five years.

Housing Choice Voucher to Homeownership Program:
Allows homebuyers to use their monthly rental assistance in
the Housing Choice Voucher program to be applied toward
a home loan payment.

Special First Mortgage Loan Programs: Offers low-interest
fixed-rate thirty-year loans for newly constructed houses for
single parent, disabled, and elderly households. Not
restricted to first-time homebuyers.

LOUISIANA

LHFA – Louisiana Housing Finance Agency, 2415 Quail Dr.,
Baton Rouge, LA 70808; LHFA.state.la.us; 225-763-8700;
888-454-2001

HOME/MRB Program Loans (Assisted and Unassisted): Low
fixed-interest-rate mortgage loan. Assistance equal to 4.5%
to 9% of mortgage loan amount will be paid at closing to
cover part of the down payment, closing costs, and prepaid
items. Unassisted loans are for those who can pay down
payment and closing costs but prefer a lower interest rate.

**CDBG/MRB Program Loans (Community Development
Block Grant):** Low fixed-interest-rate; assistance for down
payment and closing costs. Limited to eleven parishes in
designated recovery zones or on the FEMA list of damaged
properties due to Hurricane Katrina or Rita.

Teachers Assisted Program Loans: For eligible teachers, low-
interest-rate mortgages, and payments equal to 4% of the
mortgage loan paid at closing to cover part of down
payment and closing costs.

Rural Housing Development Program: Low-income families
in rural areas can receive up to $14,999 for the purchase of a
home. Partnership with USDA and Habitat for Humanity.

American Dream Down Payment Initiative (ADDI):
Provides grants up to 6% of the sales price or $10,000,
whichever is greater, in connection with the lender's first
mortgage loan.

MAINE

Maine Housing – Maine State Housing Authority, 353 Water
St., Augusta, ME 04330; MaineHousing.org; 207-626-4600;
800-452-4668

First Home Program: Low-interest fixed-rate mortgages. No
points, no down payment, extended term options available.
Most Maine households are income eligible for the
program.

Operation New Home: Low fixed-rate mortgages to veterans
and active military duty personnel. No points, no down
payment, extended term options all available. Not restricted
to first-time homebuyers, but home purchased must be used
as primary residence.

Maine American Dream Initiative Program (MADI): Helps
low-income first-time homebuyers with down payments,
closing costs, repairs, or other financing.

MARYLAND

DHCD – Maryland Department of Housing and Community
Development, 1201 W. Pratt St., Suite D, Baltimore, MD
21223; DHCD.state.md.us; 410-209-5800

Maryland Mortgage Program: Thirty- and forty-year low-
interest fixed-rate mortgage loans. Also thirty-five-year and
forty-year interest-only loan products.

CDA (Community Development Administration) Grant Assistance: Interest-only mortgage loans at below-market interest rates. Down-payment and closing-cost assistance available. Amounts can be 2% or 3% of mortgage loan, or 0% deferred loans through the Down Payment and Settlement Expense Loan Program (DSELP).

House Keys 4 Employees: DHCD will match contributions dollar-for-dollar toward down payment and closing costs from participating employers. The match is in the form of a 0% deferred loan repayable at the time of refinance, payoff, or sale of the house.

MASSACHUSETTS

MassHousing – Massachusetts Housing Finance Agency, One Beacon St., Boston, MA 02108-3110; MassHousing.com; 617-854-1000; 800-439-2370

MassAdvantage: Below market fixed-interest rates, low fees, and flexible underwriting.

MyCommunity Mortgages: For those who earn too much to qualify for a MassAdvantage loan. Not restricted to first-time homebuyers.

Home for the Brave: Affordable, no-down-payment mortgage financing for veterans, active duty military, or spouses of soldiers, sailors or marines killed while on active duty. In conjunction, grants from the Veterans Administration are available to help disabled veterans make accessibility upgrades to properties they purchase. Not restricted to first-time homebuyers.

Take the T: Transit Oriented Mortgages: No-down-payment mortgage with a low-interest rate loan intended for regular riders of public transportation. Homebuyer must show proof of this, and purchase a home near public transportation. Not restricted to first-time homebuyers.

Municipal Mortgage Program: Helps police officers, firefighters, teachers, nurses, and other public servants buy a home in the community they serve. Not restricted to first-time homebuyers.

Purchase and Rehabilitation Loans: Helps borrowers cover both the cost of purchasing a home in need of repairs, as well as the expense of rehabilitating that property.

MICHIGAN

MSHDA – Michigan State Housing Development Authority, 735 E. Michigan Ave., P.O. Box 30044, Lansing, MI 48909; Michigan.gov/mshda; 517-373-8370

Conventional 95% to 97% LTV (Loan to Value Ratio): Thirty-year fixed-rate conventional loan. Down-payment assistance available, as well as step rates and/or buy down options.

Down Payment Assistance: Zero interest, non-amortizing loan with no monthly payments, may be used for down payment, closing costs, prepaid/escrow expenses and home inspection. Loan due upon sale of property or refinancing.

Graduate Purchase Assistance: Reduced-interest-rate conventional loan program for college graduates receiving a degree within three years prior to loan application.

Down Payment Assistance Program for Persons with Disabilities: Assistance is provided in the form of a second mortgage. A 0% non-amortizing loan due on sale or refinance.

Employer Assisted Housing: MSHDA provides matching funds in a Down Payment Assistance Deferred Loan for employees of participating employers.

MINNESOTA

Minnesota Housing – Minnesota Housing Finance Agency, 400 Sibley St., Suite #300, St. Paul, MN 55101; MNhousing.state.mn.us; 651-296-8215; 800-710-8871

Minnesota Mortgage Program (MMP): Low fixed-interest-rate mortgage loans for low- to moderate-income families.

Homeownership Assistance Fund (HAF): Interest-free, deferred loan to help with down payment and closing costs.

HOME Homeowner Entry Loan Program (HOME HELP): Interest-free, deferred loan to assist with down payment and closing costs, with full repayment in the first five years; or 30% of the initial loan amount due upon maturity of the first mortgage.

Community Activity Set Aside Program (CASA): Low fixed-interest rates are available to eligible homebuyers through lenders participating in initiatives in several targeted communities around the state.

Urban Indian Housing Program: Low fixed-interest-rate mortgages to low- to moderate-income American Indian families purchasing their first home in various urban areas of Minnesota.

MISSISSIPPI

MHC – Mississippi Home Corporation, 735 Riverside Dr., Jackson, MS 39202; MShomecorp.com; 601-718-4636; 800-544-6960

Mortgage Revenue Bond Program: Lower-interest mortgage-loan rate as well as cash advance to assist with closing and down payment costs.

Mortgage Credit Certificate: Reduces the amount of federal income tax the borrower must pay, which in turn frees up income to qualify for a mortgage.

Down Payment Assistance Program: A second mortgage with a ten-year fixed-rate that matches the first-mortgage rate, to be used for down payment and closing costs.

HAT Program (Housing Assistance for Teachers): Assistance for down payment and closing costs in targeted counties. The promissory note is converted to an interest-free grant if the participant agrees to certain employment conditions. Not restricted to first-time homebuyers.

HOYO Project (Home of Your Own Program): Financial assistance for individuals with disabilities and their family members.

Habitat Loan Purchase Program: Habitat for Humanity and MHC partnership to provide housing and home financing for eligible families.

MISSOURI

MHDC – Missouri Housing Development Commission, 3435 Broadway, Kansas City, MO 64111; MHDC.com; 816-759-6600

First Place Loans: Below-market-interest rates for mortgage financing. Also may include a forgivable cash-assistance second-mortgage loan to help with down payment and closing costs.

Tax Credit Incentive: A tax-credit-advance loan program to borrow funds on a short-term basis (for help with down payment and closing costs) by advancing a portion of the anticipated tax-credit-refund amount.

Loans for Veterans: Below-market interest rates for mortgage loans for veterans or those on active duty, as well as interest-free, forgivable cash-assistance second-mortgage loans to help with down payment and closing costs.

Disaster Areas: Help for homebuyers in federally declared disaster areas, in the form of a low-interest first mortgage, as well as an interest-free, forgivable cash-assistance second mortgage for down payment and closing costs.

American Dream Down Payment Initiative Program: Down-payment and closing-cost assistance. In addition, there is a special program for rural homebuyers.

MONTANA

MDOC – Montana Department of Commerce, (Housing Division and MBOH – Montana Board of Housing), 301 S. Park, P.O. Box 200501, Helena, MT 59620-0501; Housing.mt.gov; 406-841-2840; 800-761-6264

Single Family Mortgage Program: Low-interest rates for first mortgage financing.

Mortgage Credit Certificate: Allows eligible homebuyers to receive a dollar-for-dollar reduction in their federal income taxes of up to 20% of the annual interest paid on their mortgage, to make a home purchase more affordable.

My Montana Mortgage Program: Lower-interest first-mortgage loans targeted to four groups: Native Americans, disabled, Section 8 clients, and essential workers in the fields of education, medicine, fire fighting, and law enforcement.

Neighbor Works Montana: Second-mortgage funding for down-payment and closing-cost assistance. Other down payment programs available.

Montana House: Collaboration between MBOH and various entities. Community-college students build homes with MHOB supplies that become available for modest purchase price.

Habitat for Humanity Program: Interest-free first mortgages for Habitat homebuyers.

NEBRASKA

NIFA – Nebraska Investment Finance Authority,1230 "O" St., Suite 200, Lincoln, NE 68508-1402 ; NIFA.org; 402-434-3900; 800-204-NIFA (6432)

Single Family First Home Mortgage: Below-market interest, fixed-rate, thirty-year term loan. Interest rates are adjustable. Not restricted to first-time homebuyers in target areas.

Affordable Housing Grant Program (AHP): Down-payment and closing-cost assistance in conjunction with the Single Family Mortgage Revenue Bond (MRB) Programs.

Single Family First Home Plus: Similar to the First Home Mortgage Program, except that it eliminates some of the costs and fees associated with obtaining a mortgage.

Single Family First Home Focused (Targeted Areas): Lower-interest rate and higher-income and purchase-price limits.

Bar-None Housing: Cooperative effort designed to create affordable housing for residents of rural Nebraska.

NEVADA

NHD – Nevada Housing Division, 1771 East Flamingo Road, Suite 103-B, Las Vegas, NV 89119; NVhousing.state.nv.us; 702-486-7220

First-time Homebuyer Program: Fixed-interest-rate thirty-year loans with additional assistance available for down payment and closing costs.

Teachers First Payment Subsidy Program: For teachers, below-market thirty-year fixed-interest-rate first mortgages, as well as a second-mortgage loan, which provides subsidy payments for five years and then converts to a twenty-year repayable loan.

Homeowners Rehabilitation and Down Payment Assistance: Funds available for rehabilitation and down payment for those with household income not greater than 60% of area median. Not restricted to first-time homebuyers.

NEW HAMPSHIRE

NHHFA – New Hampshire Housing Finance Authority, 32 Constitution Dr., Bedford, NH 03110; NHHFA.org; 603-472-8623; 800-649-0470

Single Family Mortgage Program: Below-market fixed rates, thirty- or forty-year terms, options with one or zero points, low down-payment requirements.

Cash Assistance for Single Family Mortgage Program: Helps borrowers defray the cost of down payment, closing costs, prepaid escrow expenses. After forty-eight months the full amount of the grant is forgiven if the mortgage has not been paid off.

Purchase/Rehab Program: Provides up to $40,000 for repairs, renovations, and improvements for borrowers obtaining a mortgage through the New Hampshire Housing Single Family Mortgage Program.

Voucher Assisted Mortgage Option: For very low-income families to purchase a home and use the Housing Choice Voucher (Section 8) as a portion of their monthly mortgage payment.

Home of Your Own Program: Provides mortgage funding and other support to assist lower-income persons with developmental disabilities.

Home Access Program: Helps low- and moderate-income borrowers to acquire a home and/or make it accessible for a permanently disabled household member.

American Dream Program: Financial assistance for down payment and closing costs for families obtaining a first mortgage through the Single Family Mortgage Program.

NEW JERSEY

HMFA – New Jersey Housing and Mortgage Finance Agency, 637 South Clinton Ave., P.O. Box 18550, Trenton, NJ 08650; State.nj.us/dca/hmfa; 609-278-7400

First-time Homebuyer and Urban Target Area Buyers: Below-market, thirty-year fixed-interest rate, low down payments.

Home Plus: A fixed-interest-rate mortgage in which home-buyers are also allowed to finance up to $15,000 toward home repairs and improvements as part of the first mortgage.

100% Financing: Provides no-down-payment, no-mortgage-insurance loans for preapproved new or rehabilitated single-family housing. Thirty-year fixed interest rate.

Smart Start: Helps families purchasing homes in Smart Growth areas by offering a second mortgage for down payment and/or closing costs. (Smart Growth is a long-term planning program by the State of New Jersey for the guidance of future growth, protection of the environment, and encouragement of compact, mixed-use development and redevelopment.)

HOPE Program: Employer Assisted Housing Program (Home Ownership Opportunities for Performing Employees). Employers guarantee 20% of the employee's loan amount.

Live Where You Work (LWYW): Home mortgage incentive program that provides low-interest mortgage loans to homebuyers purchasing homes in towns where they are employed with the goal of building stronger communities and reducing the need for cars.

Police and Fire Mortgage: Lower-interest thirty-year fixed-rate mortgages for any currently employed police officer or firefighter who is a member of the Police and Firemen's Retirement System. Not limited to first-time homebuyers.

Section 8 Home Choice Voucher: Thirty-year fixed-rate mortgage loans. Voucher payments may be applied to mortgage payments.

Transit Smart: Low-interest thirty-year fixed-rate first mortgage on properties located in Smart Growth areas, where purchasers must verify that they will be commuting to work on local public transit.

NEW MEXICO

NMMFA – New Mexico Mortgage Finance Authority, 344 4th St., SW, Albuquerque, NM 87102; NMMFA.org; 505-843-6880; 800-444-6880

MortgageSaver, MortgageSaver Zero, MortgageSaver Xtra, MortgageSaver Plus: Below-market interest rates and/or closing-cost assistance. Borrowers qualify for particular MortgageSaver programs based on household income, family size, and purchasing price. MortgageSaver is a thirty-year fixed loan; MortgageSaver Zero has no origination or discount fees; MortgageSaver Xtra features a deeply discounted interest rate for very low-income borrowers; MortgageSaver Plus includes down-payment assistance built into the loan.

HERO (Home Equity and Required Occupation): First and second mortgage used jointly to include down-payment and closing-cost assistance to household where one person is a safety worker, healthcare worker, educator, or active member of the armed forces. Not restricted to first-time homebuyers.

Payment Saver: Works with a below-market interest-rate first-mortgage loan as a second mortgage loan at 0% interest to help cover down payment and closing costs.

Helping Hand: Down-payment and closing-cost assistance for low-income families in which at least one family member has an ADA (Americans with Disabilities Act) disability.

Mortgage Booster: Second-mortgage product that provides down-payment and closing-cost assistance to borrowers who qualify for a MortgageSaver loan.

NEW YORK

SONYMA – State of New York Mortgage Agency, 641 Lexington Ave., 4th Floor, New York, NY 10022; NYhomes.org; 212-688-4000

Low-interest Rate Mortgage Program: Lower fixed-interest rate, no points, financing of up to 97% of the property.

Closing Cost Assistance Program: Assistance requires no monthly payments and is forgiven after ten years. May only be used in conjunction with a mortgage loan obtained under SONYMA programs.

Achieving the Dream Program: Provides low-income first-time homebuyers with low-down-payment-mortgage financing. Closing-cost assistance is also available for this program.

Remodel New York Program: Below-market interest-rate financing for the purchase and renovation of homes in need of improvement or repairs, financed with one mortgage.

Homes for Veterans Program: Mortgages for active-duty military, or honorably discharged or released military. Not restricted to first-time homebuyers. Closing-cost assistance also available.

ENERGY STAR Labeled Homes: Low-interest rates and closing-cost assistance for purchasers of newly constructed energy-efficient homes.

Constructive Incentive Program: Low-interest rates, no points, financing of up to 100% of property in an effort to stimulate the construction of new one- and two-family homes.

Section 8 Voucher Homeownership Mortgage Program: 4% SONYMA mortgages to Section 8 voucher recipients to help them become first-time homeowners. Closing-cost assistance also available.

DHCR – Division of Housing and Community Renewal, Hampton Plaza, 38-40 State St., Albany, NY 12207, NYsdhcr.gov; 518-473-2526; 866-275-3427

Section 8 Home Ownership Program: Voucher-assistance payments used to help families purchase and retain a home.

NORTH CAROLINA

NCHFA – North Carolina Housing Finance Agency, North Carolina Housing Finance Agency, P.O. Box 28066, Raleigh, NC 27611-8066; NCHFA.com; 919-877-5700; 800-393-0988

FirstHome Mortgage: Thirty-year fixed-rate mortgages at below-market rates.

Down Payment Assistance: Interest-free, deferred second mortgages up to $7,000 to assist with down payment and closing costs.

Second Mortgage: Deferred second mortgage loans of up to $20,000 for the purchase of newly constructed homes.

Job Loss Protection/Home Saver Program: Assistance to help you keep your home if you lose your job during the first two years of the mortgage. These funds are a second mortgage with no interest and no monthly payments, payable when you sell, transfer, or refinance the home.

Mortgage Credit Certificate: Allows mortgage interest to be claimed as a credit on federal income taxes. This saves up to $2,000 per year that can be used toward a mortgage payment.

New Homebuyer Tax Credit: Refundable tax credit of 10% of purchase price. Must be paid back over fifteen years.

Non-First-time Homebuyers: Buyers in targeted areas as well as military veterans may be eligible for the above programs even if they are not first-time homebuyers.

NORTH DAKOTA

NDHFA – North Dakota Housing Finance Agency, P.O. Box 1535, 1500 E. Capitol Ave., Bismarck, ND 58502-1535; NDHFA.org; 701-328-8080; 800-292-8621

FirstHome Program: Low-interest fixed-rate mortgages for first-time homebuyers.

HomeKey Program: Fixed-interest rate mortgage 1% below the FirstHome rate for lower- income families.

HomeAccess Program: Low-interest mortgage loans to disabled, elderly, veteran, and single-parent households. Only for purchases, but not restricted to first-homebuyers.

North Dakota Roots: Below-market interest-rate loans or market-interest-rate loans that include down-payment and closing-cost assistance for new or returning North Dakotans.

Rural Real Estate Mortgage Program: Residential real estate nonfarm mortgages guaranteed under the Rural Housing Service.

Targeted Area Loans: Low-interest-rate mortgages with the same requirements as FirstHome, but not restricted to first-time homebuyers.

Start Program: Provides affordable first mortgages and assistance with out-of-pocket cash requirements.

Down Payment and Closing Cost Assistance Program: Zero interest deferred-payment loans available to help lower-income first-time homebuyers meet their out-of-pocket cash requirements.

Approved Second Mortgage/Grant Programs (Non-NDHFA): Several nonprofit or government agencies throughout the state offer programs to assist with the down payment and closing costs of purchasing a home. Check website for approved programs.

Habitat for Humanity Loan Purchase Program: Partnership where Habitat for Humanity builds a home and sells it to a selected family, a private lender finances the purchase, and the NDHFA purchases the loan from the lender.

Homeownership Acquisition and Rehabilitation Program (HARP): NDHFA purchases and rehabilitates existing single-family homes for resale to eligible low-income homebuyers.

OHIO

OHFA – Ohio Housing Finance Agency, 57 East Main St., Columbus, OH 43215; OhioHome.org; 614-466-7970; 888-362-6432

First-time Homebuyer Program: Competitive interest rates and mortgage options on thirty-year, fixed-rate mortgage loans.

Target Area Loan Program: Helps revitalize federally designated economically distressed target areas by making first-time homebuyer products and competitive interest rates available to any qualifying buyer. Not restricted to first-time homebuyers.

Ohio Heroes Program: Offers the benefits of the First-time Homebuyer Program at a ¼% lower interest rate to active military, active reserve, and veterans; firefighters, emergency medical technicians, paramedics; healthcare workers, police officers, and teachers.

Down Payment Assistance Options: Second-mortgage loans and down-payment assistance grants to help with down payment and closing costs.

OKLAHOMA

OHFA – Oklahoma Housing Finance Agency, 100 NW 63rd, Suite 200, Oklahoma City, OK 73116; OHFA.org; 405-848-1144; 800-256-1489

OHFA Advantage: Below-market interest rates on thirty-year fixed-rate mortgage loans.

1st Gold: Down-payment and closing-cost assistance.

OHFA Shield: Fixed-rate mortgage loans and down-payment assistance for firefighters and police officers.

OHFA 4 Teachers: Fixed-rate mortgage loans and down-payment assistance for teachers.

OREGON

OHCS – Oregon Housing and Community Services, 725 Summer St., NE, Suite B, Salem, OR 97301-1266; Oregon.gov/OHCS; 503-986-2000

RateAdvantage: Below-market fixed-rate thirty-year mortgage loan to maximize home purchasing power.

CashAdvantage: Below-market fixed-interest rate on home loans, along with cash assistance equal to 5% of the loan amount to help with down payment and closing costs.

Home Purchase Assistance Program (HPAP): Down-payment and closing-cost assistance program for low-income first-time homebuyers.

Purchase Assistance Loan (PAL): Secondary loan from OHCS to help low-income first-time homebuyers with closing costs and down payment.

PENNSYLVANIA

PHFA – Pennsylvania Housing Finance Agency, 211 North Front St., Harrisburg, PA 17101-1406; PHFA.org; 717-780-3871; 800-822-1174

Keystone Home Loan Program: Low-interest thirty-year fixed-rate loans, with the highest income and purchase price limits.

Keystone Home Loan PLUS Program: Low-interest thirty-year fixed-rate loans with lower income and purchase price restrictions. Also includes eligibility for up to $2,000 in additional assistance in the Keystone PLUS Assistance Program.

Purchase Improvement Loan: Allows buyers who qualify for a Keystone Home Loan or a Keystone Home Loan PLUS to purchase and improve/repair a home within one transaction, by including between $1,000 and $15,000 with a conventional PHFA first mortgage.

HOMEstead Downpayment and Closing Cost Assistance Loan: Up to $14,999 in down payment and closing-cost assistance in the form of a no-interest second-mortgage loan. Loan is forgiven at 20% per year over five years.

Access Home Modification Program: Mortgage loans to assist persons with disabilities or who have a household member with disabilities, and are purchasing a home that needs accessibility modifications. Deferred-payment loan with no interest and no monthly payment.

Fannie Mae Community HomeChoice: Offers assistance to buyers with disabilities, or who have a household member with disabilities, who want to purchase a home and make access modifications but who do not qualify for a PHFA home purchase loan. The Community HomeChoice loan is only available when coupled with the Access Home Modification Program.

Access Down Payment and Closing Cost Assistance Program: Up to $15,000 in a no-interest loan, available only to low-income buyers who are also using the Access Home Modification Program.

RHODE ISLAND

Rhode Island Housing, 44 Washington St., Providence, RI 02903; RhodeIslandhousing.org; 401-457-1234; 800-427-5560

FirstHomes: Fixed-rate low-interest loans, thirty- to forty-year terms. Also offered are no monthly payment second mortgages for low-income homebuyers, which are not repaid until the home is sold or refinanced.

Job-loss Protection: Free job-loss Protection insurance for the first five years of a loan. Mortgage is paid for up to six months if the homebuyer loses his/her job.

Down Payment Assistance: No down payment options, or grant money, to help with closing costs and down payment.

Closing Cost Assistance: Low-interest closing cost loans to be paid back over fifteen years, or, depending on income, various types of grants, some of which do not need to be repaid.

Renovation Assistance: Home-purchase price and funds needed to make repairs available in one safe, low-interest mortgage.

Section 8 to Home Ownership Loan: Program promoting successful homeownership, using Section 8 rental vouchers to help buy a home.

SOUTH CAROLINA

SCHousing – South Carolina State Housing Finance and Development Authority, 300-C Outlet Pointe Blvd., Columbia, SC 29210; SChousing.com; 803-896-9001

First-time Homebuyers in Targeted and Non-Targeted Counties: Competitive market-fixed interest-rate mortgage loans, as well as down-payment assistance.

Single Parent Program: The borrower must be an unmarried head of household, and custodial parent or legal guardian of at least one minor child. The first-time homebuyer requirement is waived.

Individual or Family Disability Program: The borrower must be 100% permanently disabled or handicapped, or be a legal guardian of at least one dependent who is 100% permanently disabled or handicapped. The first-time homebuyer requirement is waived.

Extended Lock Program: For first-time homebuyers needing to secure a fixed-rate loan on a home that is being constructed. The borrower will be allowed a one-time rate float-down to SC State Housing's current interest rate prior to the closing date.

SOUTH DAKOTA

SDHDA – South Dakota Housing Development Authority, P.O. Box 1237, 221 S. Central Ave., Pierre, SD 57501; SDHDA.org; 605-773-3181; 800-540-4241

First-time Homebuyer Program: Below-market fixed-interest-rate mortgage loans.

Veteran's Waiver: The first-time homebuyer requirement is waived for eligible veterans, who may then obtain mortgage financing through SDHDA's First-Time Homebuyer Program.

Loan Assistance Program (LAP): Provides loans for down payment, closing-cost assistance and gap financing. LAP loans have level monthly payments and loan terms from five to ten years.

Employer Mortgage Assistance Program (EMAP): Provides down-payment and closing-cost assistance in the form of a low-interest second mortgage for homebuyers who are employed with a participating employer.

TENNESSEE

THDA – Tennessee Housing Development Authority, 404 James Robertson Pkwy., Suite 1200, Nashville, TN 37243-0900; 615-815-2200; 800-228-8432

Great Rate Program: Below-market thirty-year fixed-interest rate loan.

Great Advantage Program: Slightly higher thirty-year fixed-interest rate loan, with the addition of 2% of the loan amount available to the borrower to assist with down payment and closing costs.

Great Start Program: Slightly higher thirty-year fixed-interest rate loan with the addition of 4% of the loan amount available to the borrower to assist with down payment and closing costs.

Section 8 to Homeownership Program: Offers a mortgage subsidy to low-income families. The THDA pays the difference between the family's Total Tenant Payment and the actual monthly mortgage payment.

ADDI (American Dream Downpayment Initiative): Down-payment and closing-cost assistance.

TEXAS

TDHCA – Texas Department of Housing and Community Affairs, 221 East 11th St., Austin, TX 78701-2410; TDHCA.state.tx.us; 512-475-3800; 800-525-0657

Texas First-time Homebuyer Program: Below-market interest-rate mortgage loans. An "Unassisted Rate" loan offers the lowest interest rate and does not provide funds for down-payment and closing-cost assistance. The "Assisted Rate" loan is offered at a slightly higher interest rate and also provides grant funds of up to 5% of the mortgage amount.

Mortgage Credit Certificate (MCC) Program: Reduces a homebuyer's federal income tax obligation, thereby increasing their disposable income.

Texas Bootstrap Loan Program: Mortgage loans for very low-income families, as part of a self-help construction program. All participants are required to provide at least 60% of the labor that is necessary to construct or rehabilitate the home.

Texas Loan Star Program: Offers up to 8% of the purchase price of a home in down-payment and closing-cost assistance in the form of a repayable second-lien loan, with no money down. Not restricted to first-time homebuyers

UTAH

UHC – Utah Housing Corporation, 2479 S. Lake Park Blvd., West Valley City, UT 84120; UtahHousingcorp.org; 801-902-8200; 800-284-6950

FirstHome: Low fixed-interest-rate loans for homebuyers who are able to pay their own down payment and closing costs.

FirstHome Plus: Offers financial assistance for down payment and closing costs, in the form of a second mortgage that will have the same term as the first mortgage, but at an interest rate 1% higher.

Veterans Enhancement Program (VEP) – FirstHome: Preferred loan for veterans who are able to pay their own down payment and closing costs.

Veterans Enhancement Program (VEP) – FirstHome Plus: Offers financial assistance for down payment and closing costs, in the form of a second mortgage that will have the same term as the first mortgage but at an interest rate 1% higher.

Single Parent FirstHome: First-mortgage loans designed to assist single parents who have previously owned or co-owned their own residence and have primary custody of at least one minor dependent.

Single Parent FirstHome Plus: For applicants who also need to borrow funds for down payment and closing costs. "Sweat Equity" may also be used to assist with down payment and closing costs.

ADDI (American Dream Downpayment Initiative): Provides down-payment or closing-cost assistance in the form of interest-free loans.

VERMONT

VHFA – Vermont Housing Finance Agency, 164 St. Paul St., Burlington, VT 05401-4634; VHFA.org; 802-864-5743; 800-339-5866

MOVE – Mortgages for Vermonters:
Fixed-rate: Rates with 1 or 0 points are available for a thirty-year term.
Cash Assistance Rate: One rate option with 0 points available for a thirty-year term. Cash Assistance Rate provides borrowers with funds to be applied towards down payment

and closing costs as a second mortgage at a 0% interest rate with no monthly payments. After sixty months the Cash Assistance mortgage loan is not required to be repaid.

Manufactured Housing Program and rate options for financing for purchase of new and existing, single and double-wide mobile homes that are permanently affixed to a foundation.

HOUSE – Homeownership Opportunities Using Shared Equity: Available for homebuyers who work with a nonprofit housing organization and agree to share their home's appreciation with future buyers in exchange for purchase assistance.

Section 8 Home Ownership Program: Allows Section 8 Rental Voucher recipients to convert them into Home Ownership Vouchers. Homebuyer may also be eligible to receive assistance in meeting monthly homeownership expenses such as mortgage, taxes and insurance.

VIRGINIA

VHDA – Virginia Housing Development Authority, 601 S. Belvidere St., Richmond, VA 23220; VHDA.com; 804-782-1986; 877-VHDA-123

First-Time Homebuyer Programs: Below-market, fixed-rate thirty-year loans. There are various options including financing of closing costs and low or zero down payment.

SPARC (Sponsoring Partnerships and Revitalizing Communities): Offers interest rates lower than those of the First-Time Homebuyer Program, in conjunction with local housing organizations. Designed to address critical housing needs within communities.

HomeStride: Provides low-interest rate second mortgages of up to $25,000 to assist households in affording homeownership in identified high-cost markets.

DHCD – Virginia Department of Housing and Community Development, The Jackson Center, 501 North Second St., Richmond, VA 23219-1321; DHCD.virginia.gov; 804-371-7000

HOMEownership Down Payment Assistance Program: Offers down-payment and closing-cost assistance to low- to moderate-income homebuyers.

WASHINGTON

WSHFC – Washington State Housing Finance Commission, 1000 Second Ave., Suite 2700, Seattle, WA 98104; WSHFC.org; 206-464-7139; 800-767-4663

House Key State Bond Program: Below-market fixed-interest rate first-mortgage loan program.

House Key Plus Program: Provides down-payment and closing-cost assistance up to $10,000 in the form of a second mortgage.

HomeChoice Program: Down-payment and closing-cost assistance up to $15,000 for low- to moderate-income applicants who have a disability, or a household member with a disability.

House Key Rural Program: Second mortgage with a 3% simple interest rate. No monthly payments; balance is due when the borrower sells, pays off, or refinances the property.

House Key Veterans Program: Down-payment assistance second-mortgage program with a 3% interest rate and a ten-year loan term for veterans.

House Key Schools Program: Down-payment assistance second-mortgage program with a 3% interest rate and a ten-year loan term for educators.

WEST VIRGINIA

WVHDF – West Virginia Housing Development Fund, 814 Virginia St., East, Charleston, WV 25301; WVHDF.com; 304-345-6475; 800-933-9843

First-time Homebuyer Program: Below-market fixed-rate twenty-five to thirty-year mortgage loan. Up to 100% of the purchase price can be financed.

Secondary Market Program: Not restricted to first-time homebuyers. Offers ten-, fifteen-, twenty- or thirty-year competitive fixed-rate mortgage loans of up to 97% of the sale price of the home.

Home Ownership Assistance Program: Down-payment and closing-cost assistance loans.

Mountaineer Mortgage Credit Certificate Program (MMCC): Reduces housing expenses for homeowners through a federal tax credit based on the annual interest paid on the mortgage loan.

American Dream Down Payment Initiative (ADDI): Provides down-payment assistance to low- to moderate-income homebuyers.

HOME Leverage Loan Program (HLLP): For low- to moderate-income homebuyers, a thirty-year loan of up to $40,000. Payments are principal only in a second- or third-lien position after the first-mortgage loan.

WISCONSIN

WHEDA – Wisconsin Housing and Economic Development Authority, 201 W. Washington Ave., Suite 700, Madison, WI 53703; WHEDA.com; 608-266-7884; 800-334-6873

Home Loan: Low-cost, fixed-interest-rate first-mortgage loan, up to thirty-year term, low down payment, job-loss protection in the event of involuntary unemployment.

Home Loan for Veterans: Offers long-term, low-cost fixed-interest rate financing to military veterans purchasing a home. Includes low down payment and job-loss protection. Not restricted to first-time homebuyers.

Easy Close: Low-cost, fixed-interest-rate fifteen-year loan for assistance with down payment and closing costs.

Partnership Neighborhood Initiative: Offers down-payment assistance to homebuyers in targeted neighborhoods. Includes minimal cash at closing, low-payment loans to assist with down payment, and job-loss payment protection.

Partnership for Homeownership: Provides affordable home financing for rural residents, including no down payment; low-cost fixed-interest rate; no private mortgage insurance requirement; and financing of all fees.

Rural Initiative Down Payment Assistance: Down-payment assistance for buyers in specific rural markets, in the form of a 0% interest, no monthly payment, five-year forgivable grant of $5,000 per household.

Major Rehabilitation Loan: Provides thirty-year fixed-rate financing to purchase and rehabilitate an existing home, or to refinance and rehabilitate a current home. Not restricted to first-time homebuyers.

WYOMING

WCDA – Wyoming Community Development Authority, 155 N. Beech, Casper, WY 82601; WyomingCDA.com; 307-265-0603

Standard Homebuyer Program: Provides thirty-year mortgage loans at below-market interest rates.

Down Payment Loan Program: Provides assistance with down payment and closing costs in the form of a second mortgage on the property of up to $13,000. Terms may be from one to ninety-six months.

Homebuyer Assistance Program: Funding for thirty-year deferred loans. Eligible homebuyers may receive assistance for down payment and closing costs as well. If the borrower lives in the property for thirty years, the loan is forgiven.

Spruce Up Wyoming Programs: Financing for purchase and rehabilitation of substandard houses. Various options are available, including below-market interest rates, home purchase, and rehabilitation or home refinance and rehabilitation. Not restricted to first-time homebuyers.

HOME Run Program: Assistance to first-time homebuyers by providing an interest-rate subsidy if they purchase a newly constructed home.

State Real Estate Commission Websites

To Check Realtor Licenses and Complaints:

ALABAMA
AREC.state.al.us

ALASKA
DCED.state.ak.us/occ/prec.htm

ARIZONA
RE.state.az.us

ARKANSAS
State.ar.us/arec/arecweb.html

CALIFORNIA
DRE.ca.gov

COLORADO
DORA.state.co.us/real-estate/

CONNECTICUT
CT.gov/dcp/cwp/view.asp?a=1624&Q=276076

DELAWARE
DPR.delaware.gov/boards/realestate/index.shtml

DISTRICT OF COLUMBIA
APP.DCRA.dc.gov/information/build_pla/occupational/real_estate/index.shtm

FLORIDA
MyFloridaLicense.com/dbpr/re/frec.html

GEORGIA
GREC.state.ga.us

HAWAII
Hawaii.gov/dcca/quicklinks/online/business_online

IDAHO
IdahoRealEstateCommission.com

ILLINOIS
IDFPR.com

INDIANA
IN.gov/pla/real.htm

IOWA
State.ia.us/government/com/prof/sales/home.html

KANSAS
AccessKansas.org/krec/

KENTUCKY
KREC.us/krec.gov/

LOUISIANA
LREC.state.la.us/

MAINE
State.me.us/pfr/professionallicensing/index.shtml

MARYLAND
DLLR.state.md.us/license/occprof/recomm.html

MASSACHUSETTS
Mass.gov. Go to "For Residents," click on "Housing." Then click on "Check a Professional License."

MICHIGAN
Michigan.gov/dleg/ Click on "How Do I Find the Licensing Division?"

MINNESOTA
Commerce.state.mn.us. Go to Go to "License Look-Up Tool."

MISSISSIPPI
MREC.state.ms.us/

MISSOURI
PR.mo.gov/realestate.asp

MONTANA
MT.gov/DLI/BSD/license/bsd_boards/rre_board/board_page.asp

NEBRASKA
NREC.state.ne.us

NEVADA
Red.state.nv.us/realestate/re_home.htm

NEW HAMPSHIRE
NH.gov/nhrec

NEW JERSEY
State.nj.us/dobi/division_rec/index.htm

NEW MEXICO
RLD.state.nm.us/RealEstateCommission/index.html

NEW YORK
DOS.state.ny.us/lcns/realest.html

NORTH CAROLINA
NCREC.state.nc.us

NORTH DAKOTA
RealEstatend.org

OHIO
com.Ohio.gov/real

OKLAHOMA
OK.gov/OREC

OREGON
Oregon.gov/REA/index.shtml

PENNSYLVANIA
DOS.state.pa.us/bpoa/cwp/view.asp?a=1104&Q=433107

RHODE ISLAND
DBR.state.ri.us/divisions/commlicensing/realestate.php

SOUTH CAROLINA
LLRonline.com/POL/REC

SOUTH DAKOTA
State.sd.us/sdrec

TENNESSEE
Tennessee.gov/commerce/boards/trec

TEXAS
TREC.state.tx.us

UTAH
RealEstate.utah.gov

VERMONT
VTprofessionals.org/opr1/real_estate

VIRGINIA
DPOR.virginia.gov/dporweb/reb_main.cfm

WASHINGTON
DOL.wa.gov/business/realestate

WEST VIRGINIA
WVREC.org

WISCONSIN
DRL.wi.gov/index.htm

WYOMING
RealEstate.state.wy.us

Websites with First-Time Homebuyer Advice

Credit Counseling Network: creditcounselingnetwork.org

Fannie Mae: fanniemae.com/homepath/homebuyers/buyingahome.jhtml?&p=Home+Buyers

Freddie Mac: homesteps.com/homeshoppers.htm

HUD: hud.gov/buying

National Association of Realtors: realtor.com/home-finance/buyers-basics/home-buyers-basics.aspx

National Association of Realtors: realtor.org/realtororg.nsf/Pages/PrepHomeownership

National Foundation for Credit Counseling (to find credit counselor): NFCC.org

National Foundation for Credit Counseling (for buying advice): debtadvice.org

Neighbor Works: nw.org/network/training/homeownership/Homebuyingguides.asp

Canadian Home Financing Programs

*Tax rebate and down payment assistance programs change frequently due to legislative adjustments, so check each web site for the most up-to-date information.

FEDERAL GOVERNMENT HOMEBUYERS PLAN

cra-arc.gc.ca/formspubs/tpcs/hm_byrs-eng.html
800/959-8281

RRSP Homebuyers Plan (HBP)

First-time homebuyers and homebuyers with a disability may borrow up to $25,000 from their Registered Retirement Savings Plan to buy or build a home which must become their primary residence. (A first-time homebuyer cannot have owned a home within the previous four years.) If both spouses qualify for the HBP plan they can each withdraw up to $25,000 for a total of $50,000. The money must be repaid within fifteen years. Typically paid back by depositing one-fifteenth of the amount borrowed each year. Any amount not repaid after fifteen years will be subject to income tax over the following year.

FEDERAL GOVERNMENT FIRST-TIME HOMEBUYERS TAX CREDIT

cra-arc.gc.ca/gncy/bdgt/2009/fqhbtc-eng.html
800/959-8281

First-time Homebuyers Tax Credit (HBTC)

A non-refundable tax credit, based on an amount of $5,000, for first-time homebuyers (or homebuyers with a disability or buying a home to live with someone with a disability) who buy a home after January 27, 2009. (A first-time homebuyer cannot have owned a home within the previous four years.) The HBTC is calculated by multiplying the lowest personal income tax rate for the year (15% in 2009) by $5,000. For 2009, the credit will be $750. Check the website for updates.

BRITISH COLUMBIA

gov.bc.ca/sbr Bulletin PTT 004
800/663-7867

First-time Homebuyers Program

Some first-time buyers may qualify for a property transfer tax exemption if they have lived in British Columbia for 12 consecutive months, have never owned a principal residence anywhere in the world and have never received a first-time buyers exemption or refund. The property must be the principal residence, less than 1.24 acres and cost less than $425,000.

New Brunswick Home Ownership Program

gnb.ca/0017/housing/homeownership-e.pdf

Questions should be directed to regional housing office of the Department of Social Development in each area:
   Acadian Peninsula: 866/441-4149
   Chaleur: 866/441-4341
   Edmundston: 866/441-4245
   Fredericton: 866/441-4249
   Miramichi: 866/441-4246
   Moncton: 866/426-5191

Restigouche: 866/441-4245
Saint John: 866/441-4340

Home Ownership Program

Assistance in the form of a repayable loan for 25% of the purchase price of the home or up to $50,000 (not to exceed 50% of the total house costs) if building a house. The loan will be repaid over 25 years at 0% interest for households with incomes under $25,000; for each $1,000 of adjusted income above $25,000 the interest rate will increase by 0.5% until it equals the provincial borrowing rate. Loans are limited to households with incomes below $40,000 who are able to obtain financing for the rest of the home purchase or home building costs. Borrowers must be first-time buyers and residents for at least one year of New Brunswick.

NORTHWEST TERRITORIES

nwthc.gov.nt.ca/pgm_PATH.html
866/956-9842

Providing Assistance for Territorial Homeownership (PATH)

Assistance in the form of a forgivable loan for the purchase or construction of a home, with the forgiveness period dependent on the amount of assistance provided. Assistance is provided in increments based on applicant's income, family size and the community's Core Need Income Thresholds (CNIT). To qualify, applicants must be 19 or older, lived in the Northwest Territories for three years including one year in the community of application, income must be below the CNIT, applicant must have a Core housing need, be able to obtain additional funding from a financial institution, have sufficient income to pay for all housing costs without spending more than 30% of income, not have owned a home within the previous five years and complete the Solutions to Educate People (STEP) courses.

Homeownership Entry Level Program (HELP)

Provides assistance to prospective homebuyers through a lease on a Northwest Territories Housing Corporation property. Applicants pay 20% of their gross income toward rent and shelter costs such as power and water. After a successful two-year lease period, tenants are eligible for an equity contribution towards the home purchase. Applicants must be able to pay for all approved shelter costs using 20% or less of their income while renting, must complete STEP courses, have a Core Housing Need, income below the CNIT for the community, be over 19, have lived in the Northwest Territories for at least three years with one continuous year in the community of application.

NOVA SCOTIA

Gov.ns.ca/coms/housing/homeowner/FamilyModestHousing.html

Questions and applications should be directed to the Housing Services office of the nearest Department of Community Services.

Eastern Region (Cape Breton, Sydney): 800/567-2135
Northern Region (New Glasgow): 800/933-2101
Central Region (Halifax): 800/774-5130
Western Region (Middleton): 800/564-3483
Truro District Office: 866/525-5454
Amherst District Office: 902/667-1161
Bridgewater District Office: 800/278-2144

Family Modest Housing Program

Designed to provide lower and middle-income families with funds to buy or build modest housing, a mortgage of up to $70,000 is available with interest rates set at loan approval and fixed for five years. Loan must be paid back within 25 years. Applicants must have total household income under $50,000 annually, cannot currently own adequate housing, must have a favorable credit rating and be able to repay the mortgage and have an established work history with at least one year with the same employer.

ONTARIO

Ontario.ca/revenue
866/668-8297

Land Transfer Tax Refunds

First-time homebuyers may be eligible for a refund of up to $2,000 for the land transfer tax paid on a resale home or new construction. Taxpayers must be at least 18, occupy the home as a principal residence and cannot have owned a home anywhere in the world.

New Housing Rebate

Buyers of newly constructed homes purchased as a principal residence may qualify for a tax rebate of 75% of the provincial portion of the sales tax payable on the purchase of a new home, up to $24,000.

QUEBEC

habitation.gouv.qc.ca/en/programmes/renovation_quebec.html

From the above site consumers can find links to home-ownership programs in each municipality. Links are in French.
Montreal
Habitermontreal.qc.ca
514/872-4630

Home Ownership Program

First-time buyers can receive financial grants for the purchase of a newly constructed home up to $180,000 for households without children and up to $235,000 for households with at least one child under 18 on the date of purchase. The grants range from $6,500 to $7,500. Property value limits and grants are also available on existing properties from $296,000 to $455,000 that have two to five units. Applicants must now have owned a residential property in Quebec over the past five years and the home must be the applicant's principal residence.

YUKON

community.gov.yk.ca/pdf/Home_Owner_Grant_EN_web.pdf
800/661-0408

Yukon Home Owner's Grant

Homeowners who have paid their property taxes on their primary residence are eligible for a grant of 50% of the general taxes up to a maximum of $450 per household. Homeowners can apply through the web site for the grant and may deduct the grant from their taxes.

Canadian Real Estate Agencies to Search for License Compliance/Complaints

Real Estate Council of Alberta
reca.ca

Real Estate Council of British Columbia
recbc.ca/licensing/jurisdiction.htm

The Manitoba Securities Commission
msc.gov.mb.ca/real_estate/index.html

New Brunswick
New Brunswick Department of Justice
gnb.ca/0062/index.htm

Government of Newfoundland and Labrador Consumer and Commercial Affairs
gs.gov.nl.ca/cca/fsr/real-estate

Government of the Northwest Territories Municipal and Consumer Affairs
maca.gov.nt.ca/operations/consumer_affairs/tips/who_are_we/

Nova Scotia Department of Business and Consumer Services
gov.ns.ca/snsmr/business

Real Estate Council of Ontario
reco.on.ca

Prince Edward Island Community Services
gov.pe.ca/index.php3?number=1024655

Association des Courtiers et Agents Immoboliers due Quebec
acaiq.com

Saskatchewan Real Estate Commission
srec.ca/

Government of Yukon Department of Community Services
community.gov.yk.ca/consumer/pl.html

Canadian Websites with Homebuyer Information

Canada Mortgage and Housing Corporation
cmhc-schl.gc.ca/en/co/buho/index.cfm

Federal government buy or rent calculator
ic.gc.ca/eic/site/oca-bc.nsf/eng/ca01821.html

Web site with first time homebuyer information geared to Canada
firsttimebuyers.ca

Multiple Listing Service for Canada with general information and help finding a Realtor
mls.ca/splash.aspx

Canadian Real Estate Association with general information and help finding a Realtor and properties
realtor.ca/splash.aspx

Buyers Guide from ACAIQ
woapp.acaiq.com/PDF/An/Buyer_Guide.pdf

First-time homebuyers guide from Re/Max Western Canada
remax-western.ca/first-time-buyers-guide

First time homebuyers guide from Canada Trust
tdcanadatrust.com/mortgages/buyingfirst.jsp

About the Author

Michele Lerner is a respected and established real estate reporter with two decades of experience. Her work can be seen regularly in the "Friday Home Guide" of the *Washington Times*, *Urban Land* magazine, the National Association of Real Estate Investment Trusts' *Real Estate Portfolio* magazine, and on BankRate.com. She writes regularly for Realtor association magazines in Virginia, Massachusetts, Pennsylvania, New Jersey, Maryland, and Florida. Her daily blog on residential real estate can be found on Examiner.com. She lives with her husband in Washington, D.C. They frequently visit with their two daughters in New York City. Visit MicheleLerner.com